T0368494

WILDERNESS WONDERINGS

HOW I FOUND SPIRIT IN STILLNESS

REV. LARRY GRUBB

WITH

MELINDA FOLSE

Balboa Press books may be ordered through booksellers or by contacting:

Balboa Press
A Division of Hay House
1663 Liberty Drive
Bloomington, IN 47403
www.balboapress.com
844-682-1282

ISBN: 979-8-7652-4287-2 (sc)
979-8-7652-4288-9 (hc)
979-8-7652-4289-6 (e)

Library of Congress Control Number: 2023911058

Print information available on the last page.

Balboa Press rev. date: 07/12/2024

BALBOA.PRESS
A DIVISION OF HAY HOUSE

DEDICATION:

*For Patty, my loving, creative,
and supportive wife of sixty-four years*

TABLE OF CONTENTS

ACKNOWLEDGMENTS:

I humbly thank:

Melinda Folse for her tireless efforts to take my journal scribblings and shape them into *Wilderness Wonderings*.

My two daughters Leticia Martin and Cindy Stroud for their dedicated support in this endeavor, and their patient, generous spouses who kept the lights on while their wives came to my aid.

First United Methodist Church and Dr. Tim Bruster for allowing me to step away from my ministerial responsibilities for three months to experience this sabbatical.

AUTHOR'S NOTE

I prepare this document of my personal journey of transformation into that which I feel God gifted me within this life.

First, I share them in an effort to keep my own fire burning; if another may gain profit, thank our Source! And second, I share this because of what I profoundly believe.

If another finds aid in it, I humbly share it, with the realization that these are the thoughts that came to me in the wilderness. I do not claim them for my own—only as "gifts for the journey."

I share these humble thoughts, not for accolades, but thinking that perhaps some of them may stimulate thought and action in others, as they certainly did in me!

—L.G.

PROLOGUE

"Can I see your identification?"

My mind, racing ahead to the excitement of finally getting this long-awaited journey underway, hit the brakes.

"What?" I said, looking blankly at the ticket agent. Then reality dawned. "Oh! Right!" I said, reaching into the pocket where my wallet always stayed.

Coming up empty and perplexed, I began the pat-down of all the other pockets I owned, including those on the outside of my suitcase and carry-on bag.

"I'm sorry," I began, still searching, panic growing. "I know it's here somewhere." I replayed my departure preparations in my mind, a mind already frazzled by disentangling myself from my over-packed existence as a counseling pastor of a bustling metropolitan church.

Grappling with the understanding that my wallet was not with me—and that there was nowhere else to look—I added, "Let me just call my family to see if maybe I left it at home."

Reaching then for my cell phone, I experienced a horrifying replay of the wallet search. Dumbfounded, I shrugged, raising both hands, palms up, to the unimpressed ticket agent.

She waited.

I stared back at her, as if she might somehow hold the secret to solving this conundrum.

She didn't.

"Um, maybe I could use your phone?" I asked, hesitant.

Expressionless, she handed her phone across the counter to me. I held the receiver in my hand and in that moment realized I no longer knew anyone's phone number. Some phones are too smart for their own good. Turns out, though, that 1-411 can still give you someone's phone number!

Several hours of fretting and a rebooked flight later caused a long, unanticipated overlay that necessitated reworking my ground transportation arrangements once I landed. I settled, utterly exhausted, into my airplane seat. The flight to Philadelphia was uncomfortably full, but it was as close as they could get me to my original destination. I was so grateful to be on my way that I didn't even care.

My frantic 5:45 a.m. distress call had gotten my daughter Cindy out of the shower, who then called her husband Warren who, with my wife Patty, was by then nearly back home from dropping me at the airport. Patty had been her usual sweet, reassuring self, and there had not been a grumpy word from any of them about having to go back to the house to retrieve my wallet and phone from the kitchen table where I absentmindedly set them on my last trip through the kitchen to get a bottle of water.

After retrieving the items, we repeated our goodbyes, and I returned to the ticket counter to re-book my flight. Now, at last, I could settle down and return to my excited anticipation of whatever lay ahead in those woods.

What a family. Besides Patty, our daughters Cindy (and son-in-law Warren) and Leticia (and son-in-law Rob), and our son Paul (and his wife Suzanne) offered amazing, unquestioning support for this three-month odyssey that none of us was certain I would survive. I knew well that three months alone in the remote North Maine Woods with no communication, no electricity, no running water, and no transportation was dangerous for a man of nearly eight decades.

I didn't say it to them—and we didn't speak of it, per se—but I knew I was prepared for the possibility of dying in those woods. But I think we all also knew that for me not to go—and to continue to live in the extreme stress as I had been carrying for decades was a death sentence of its own.

I needed transformation. Redemption. A direct re-connection with the Source of all being. And somehow, I knew I would find God, myself, and more in those primitive woods.

CHAPTER 1

I am here in the North Woods of Maine for three months (July through September) without transportation or phone connections. Communication companies don't know this place exists. It is a quiet wilderness around an old lodge established in 1926 and unused now. There's no electricity for anyone up here in this part of Maine, no paved roads, no 7-Eleven, no gas, or food for 30 miles. The closest drinking water is five miles away from a natural spring. My food source was largely canned and non-perishable items, most of which I purchased in my initial grocery run upon arriving in Maine. I did not have to hunt or kill for food. People were very kind and generous to one another when it came to supplies.

Now I have my opportunity to be alone, in total silence, in a sanctuary of forest, water, and all manner of wildlife, to carve out a life for myself. I'm in a foreign, isolated territory and I totally depend on Divine grace from my Source for survival.

The Wild Wilderness of North Maine

~ ~ ~

"Patty, God lives here!" I said nearly 10 years ago as we drove along that spectacular rocky, unique, beautiful, mystifying shoreline. "I've *got* to come back to Maine for one or two weeks just to absorb the uniqueness of this unusual state, and especially the coastline."

When the church we served together gave my wife Patty and me a nice cash retirement gift, we used it to go to New England. We wanted to absorb the wonder of nature as she started her journey toward winter sleep. There were many glowing stories from others who had been there; we just had to see it for ourselves. After spending a full month there, we declared it to be all we expected—and much more!

One of the significant "much more" moments was Otter Point on the south end of one of the peninsulas of Maine. I spent a couple of hours sitting on that rocky shore, listening to the waves hit its mighty granite boulders. The variety of aquatic birds also intrigued me as they each danced their dance and graced the airways.

I sat with a pen and notepad as inspiration flowed through me as I had never experienced before. At the end of this historic and transforming moment, I got back in the car where Patty had been patiently sitting and waiting for me. I assume she was also saying, "when is he going to get off that rock?"

~ ~ ~

I began planning my trip back as soon as I got home. Our Internet search for a place we could return to and enjoy an expanding dream revealed a plethora of places. We soon learned that there are more summer homes and cottages in Maine than any other state we found.

Just one problem. The cost! Anywhere from one to four thousand dollars a week. United Methodist Ministers don't have that kind of retirement, so we decided to go to Plan B: find a contact who knows Maine and see if we could find a bargain!

First, I went to our good friend and beloved, retired bishop who was living in Fort Worth. Because he had been spending his summers in Maine for 20 years, I figured he surely had "connections." He was delighted to hear about my interest in returning to Maine and provided me with maps, brochures, articles, and all kinds of information about places to go and things to see. We pursued several options over the next several years, but nothing seemed to fit!

Then I remembered another friend who was an assistant to a bishop in Houston who owns a nice place on the coast of Maine. New excitement surged, and my friend made repeated attempts to reach this bishop but for whatever reason, got no response.

Then two other friends we had cherished since the 1960s who lived in Albany, New York, offered to use their network to see if they could help us out—another dead end.

On a last-ditch whim, I reached out to a good friend of the Methodist conference, a lay leader who had a place on the coast of Maine to see if that might be an option. No luck.

By then I had pushed, shoved, bugged, and searched diligently for a way to return to that coast of Maine for 10 years with no luck. Right then I decided, "I can die without a return trip to Maine. If it works out, fine. If not, I am fine with that, too!"

Perhaps I should have started there. Within a year's time another friend and church member moved to Maine and married a woman who owned an unoccupied cabin in the woods there.

"Larry, it's all yours!" he said. "You can use it 365 days a year, free!"

Just another reminder—when we try to do it alone, it ends in frustration. When we cooperate with the universe, God/our Source, unbelievable things unfold. Now, instead of one or two weeks, I had an open invitation for any time of year, for as long as I wanted to stay, and at no charge!

~ ~ ~

As they say, when something seems too good to believe, it probably is. By the time my return trip to Maine became a reality, the cabin promised was being used for storage. To his credit, however, my friend offered me the use of his pop up travel trailer that I could park at a camp on the shore of Nicatous Lake—65 miles north of Bangor. I later learned that many cabins there are occupied by families enjoying time together, others are filled with couples and singles. Five camps with sandy beaches on the west side of this part of the lake, before the narrows, and four camps on the east side. Nicatous Lake is actually three larger lakes separated by two different narrows, all passable by boat.

After driving me to my campsite from the airport in Bangor, my friend and I set up my borrowed pop-up camper by the lake, under a canopy of tall and mighty hemlock trees. I unloaded all the supplies, books, clothing, and electronics I can't use.

Pine and fir tree forest all around, solid growth. My camper is near the water's edge and well camouflaged by a line of young fir trees between me and the lake, which is about a 40-foot slope to the water. The camper provided protection from the elements and mosquitoes who love to feast on me.

The lake is deep blue, some 15 miles long, and a solid forest of maples, pines, and fir trees. Several islands, water locked where summer vacationers have cabins you can reach only by boat. From my campsite, I can see and hear boaters as they come in from an island to get supplies and leave a few hours later. About 150 yards beyond my "scene" are the two principal docks for people to put their boats in water, so I'll get a close look at a vast variety of people, crafts, supplies, dogs, equipment, canoes, and kayaks that all go to some islands in the lake, only access being water.

My friend departed for home, and I spent the rest of the day sleeping and recuperating from the trip and activity. I read some with much sharper insight and awareness in this peaceful Garden of Eden setting. To bed at dark.

My new home in Maine, near Nicatous Lake

≈ ≈ ≈

How does God work in human life? More importantly, in my life?

I've been asking that question most of my life, without satisfactory answers.

Jesus, Paul, and a cadre of other mentors in my life found they had to spend time alone, in total silence, to answer this question. I've attempted it, but found it is tough for me to be still and do nothing for very long without going crazy.

After 77 years, it hit me profoundly: "Larry, this is the key to the Kingdom of God! This is the answer to how to be God's person in the world."

Giving in, I said, "OK, God."

Back home, years ago, I practiced in small snippets of time to begin to learn how to be alone, in silence.

Then came the urge. "I need more than a few minutes a day." The decision to step out of my comfort zone directed my next steps. I've come to the wilderness (where the Hebrews, the prophets, and our Master went to find God), to spend three entire months alone, in silence. Without direct communication or easy transportation to escape, I will depend completely on the Source of all life, raw and bare.

CHAPTER 2

Abundant firewood gathered from fallen trees and branches

'm in a small, one-family, one-camper spot, with an almost built-to-regulation carport. There is a commercial seat like you sit on, a square box about two feet square, covered on three sides with half-inch hardware cloth and a solid three-quarter-inch plywood front, set over a small gully where water would run off in a heavy rain, of which they have few here. I have a really nice fire pit, built with granite rocks and sand surrounding them to form the frame above ground. I have an oversupply of wood, as you can imagine. It's unlawful to cut anything alive, but the forest is full and thick with fallen trees and branches from the heavy snows of winter.

My first (and only!) encounter with a black bear here in the wilderness of the North Maine Woods happened early this morning, probably between 3:00 and 4:00 a.m. I was sitting in a lawn chair beside my huge pit fire that was really blazing in the early stages of the fire.

I hear a deep grunt/groan from far out in the forest that piqued my interest (and initial concern). Then, about ten minutes later, I hear the same noise, this time much closer, much louder, and, I assumed, very close to my isolated camp.

For some strange reason I felt no fear as I strategized, sitting there quietly by my fire, "How will I handle this situation, should the bear choose to come and visit me?"

I was processing and strategizing alongside the following thoughts:

This is peak berry season, a bear's favorite diet.

I am living in a virtual natural garden of these lush fruits—blueberries, strawberries, raspberries, and later the cranberries.

Usually, bears won't attack humans unless they are hungry.

I talked to several old-timer Mainers who lived with these bears for years. My best resource was a man who has lived about half a mile from my camp, in these same woods, some 38 years as of last year. They all said that these bears are shy of humans. They will still attack, but only if hungry or if a mama bear has her cubs nearby, or if you disrupt them at their food source.

So, I felt safe at this point. I had a huge fire roaring, and I assumed, rightly or wrongly, that this would be a deterrent. I guess it was!

Also, the berries were a deterrent, apparently more delicious than he thought I would be!

~ ~ ~

I spent my first full day of retreat reading, writing, exploring the forest, and tuning into the symphony and sources in this pristine beauty. God and life provides an abundance of flowers in God's garden, whether or not humans ever enjoy them.

I've had some wonderful study and quiet time—reading Henry David Thoreau's 150th anniversary of *Walden*—graciously given for this trip to Thoreau's world. It deepened my appreciation of the forest, water, and what is really essential for quality life—he got it.

I read and meditated on daily reading for July 9th in Celtic Daily Prayers—readings that come from the North Umbria community of Ireland. Rich, good food for thought to deepen my spirit life and seek a clearer understanding of who God is.

~ ~ ~

There is an abundance of moose, deer, bears, porcupines, skunks, grouse, tree squirrels, and many more special creatures of the forest. Some I've seen, some I don't want to see except at a distance. There is a premiere moose habitat on the lake cove I am on, so hopefully I can encounter some of them.

I saw a great blue heron—they measure body length of over three feet and have a wingspan of six feet. That feller was searching for lunch near my shore, as I was eating my lunch. I watched him for about 15 minutes move like a snail through the water, searching for whatever he was searching for. I distracted myself to get my bird book to make sure I had him identified correctly.

There are beavers with a lodge just off my shore. I saw seven magnificent Canada geese with brilliant color and markings flying in at low altitude, straight at me, and landing about 200 yards from me. They immediately began a scrumptious dinner, feeding for about 30 minutes. They have enormous bodies to fill. When they finished, they swam to shore half a block from me. Beavers waddled up the shore, preened themselves for a while and put in for the night. It was fun watching those long-necked geese bobbing away, going after the fish they were eating. It was fascinating as they continuously kept their heads bobbing above their long necks. This entire trip to Maine was worth that scene!

There are salmon (fresh Atlantic variety), Pike, large brown and rainbow trout, big black bass, and many more in these waters. It is a fishing paradise. However, only the truly dedicated and hearty anglers make it up here. There are a few who make it to this spot. I like this. It preserves my privacy.

~ ~ ~

The unity in creation—every single bit of it. Scripture speaks of oneness with creation. I've read and believed it all my life.

Questions come along in this 20th and 21st century and confirm it in many magnificent ways that explore our abilities to comprehend. Lao-Tzu understood it deeply and intimately, and I've spent time daily seeking to unwrap this truth from 2,500 years ago in the Tao.

So how did unity of creation come more alive for me in Maine?

First, there was the peace I made with mosquitoes. I've hated these pests most of my life and have often questioned, "How do they fit into creation that is 'very, very good?'"

I got my answer, at least partially, in Maine. And I truly came to love these little fellows. I finally realized something I've known for many years—they are a very important part of the food chain for some of these little birds I love to watch and listen to their songs of praise.

So, as I sat in my camper and watched these little guys try to get to me, I realized I was really just juicy bait for them! I praise God for them and love them for the purpose I came to see, and thanked God for screens that keep them away from me for maximum comfort.

God's splendid creation.

What kind of ingenuity or creativity or intuition do these little fellows have to find the one small crack in my door, invade my privacy, and set up for battle with me? Sometimes they win, sometimes I win this battle. In awe of God's and mosquitoes' great mystery to me.

Our wisdom, creativity, and intuition must be far superior to theirs. So, now I'm confronted with the challenge, "Am I using it all as well as they?"

And consider the hummingbird. One pair of wings for forward and one for reverse, and they can change gears faster than I can blink my eyes. They can remain still in flight and move at 60 mph in two seconds. What engineering! They must be some of the most exquisitely engineered birds alive!

~ ~ ~

Third day at camp, it's cloudy with periodic light rain all day. High of 72. Any movement on my part drenches me in sweat. I must have 100 percent ocean moving through the atmosphere. The still and quiet have been delicious and invited me to do more of the same inside me.

It is a strange awareness to me that the quieter I get on the inside, the more exhausted I feel. So, I have slept most of the day, nibbling a bit of food now and then. I had chicken and mixed veggies for lunch.

Very few people have appeared today for supplies and one boat went out fishing for a while. As they were leaving, a Jeep of four men and a big boxer stopped. They must have visited for over an hour. They came out of the woods, so may have wanted a change in social discourse. I asked them if they lived there and one burly, heavily bearded fellow said, "When we want to!"

I had a small walk, and it was too humid! Just as my grandma used to do for hours on her front porch, I just sat in a lawn chair, but I only lasted for 30-45 minutes. I guess I have some conditioning toward BEING I must practice before I can endure such activity (or inactivity) for hours, but I am making progress. Today, every time my head said, "go read something," my heart said, "Larry, can't you let yourself just be?"

~ ~ ~

How do I envision myself at the end of September?

Quiet and peaceful throughout my body, mind, and spirit. Carrying this new G.O.D. into my activities—remaining quiet within.

Deeply motivated to live on the divine impulse in each action of my life.

Deeply empowered to become God's person in my world, taking full responsibility for any action within and outside.

Being is my center naturally and unconsciously.

Much more aware of my pervasive pride and ego motivation and transforming them to Authentic Self, humble, grateful, and of service to others.

CHAPTER 3

One of the big questions I went to Maine to seek an answer to: Is God a what or a who?

I've believed most of my life that God is a who. I've argued this vehemently with a District Superintendent I had from 1969 to 1973, a deep, creative thinker, a very devout, lifelong Christian, who believes God is a what.

I've argued this point with her from the time we started this debate until about two years ago when she said, "enough is enough! I'm through dialoguing about this issue!"

For the past two years, I have moved closer to her position. I see it having huge implications for our faith, our gospel, and the quality of life we live. I'm up against a mystery that is beyond my ability to understand or define.

Am I ever bored with this line of questioning? Never! How does one get bored when searching for the unsearchable? I can only be a blind man, touching an elephant and attempting to tell you what an elephant is!

~ ~ ~

Overcast mornings on Nicatous Lake

I'm awakening each day at dawn and catnapping until the sun is up. My mornings have been overcast so far, unfolding slow, easy, and relaxed. After my coffee and a little breakfast, I enjoyed a nice short walk to a pristine lake at the end of a logging trail. This morning I stood four feet from a small sparrow-like bird that was eating light gravel for five minutes. He was dark brown with a head like a quail, tan stripes running the length of his body.

The island and lakeshore are solid pine and fir, with clear blue water. These North Maine Woods remain unchanged from Thoreau's days of exploring here. No electricity. Roads all dirt and often rough, with only a few people. This is incredible beauty!

Today I enjoyed a friendly visit with a fellow named Brad I met on my walk. He was splitting wood but took the time to tell me more about the area, and he promised a boat ride to some islands in near future. Some islands are owned by families. Brad is going to loan me a book on the history of this camp, named Porter Point Camp, established in the mid-20s by an airline pilot who retired and wanted to create a recreation area in these magnificent North Maine Woods. I also learned the lake I am on has salmon, pike, and two kinds of trout, brown and rainbow, and bass. Salmon are the hardest to catch and the best eating. The lake is 12 miles long, has multiple islands, is 50-feet deep at the deepest, and averages 25 feet.

On today's walk I also met a family of four who are here for a week. They live in Denver and will move into a cabin near me on Tuesday. Then I met the daughter of the camp owner and her family of three. They are quiet types, so not very conversational, and they are very nice. It gives me some comfort to know that even as I choose to isolate myself in these woods and feel as if I'm all alone with God and nature, there are people around—we're all here to absorb the wonders of this natural world, set apart from the frenetic pace and realities many if not most of us came here to escape. Being in these woods is a choice we have all made, and whether residents who tend to keep to themselves or vacationers here and gone, I am only as alone as I need to be, which is just fine with me.

After my morning walk to explore the wonders of these beautiful woods, I am ready to settle down to my studies and meditations in nature, trying to listen for the voice of God within me.

So far I have I studied and written my reflections on Bible readings in Mark, Celtic Devotional readings, and some deep insights I found in *11 Days at the Edge: One Man's Spiritual Journey into Evolutionary Enlightenment* in which author Michael Wombacher reflects on Andrew Cohen's visionary spiritual paradigm of human transformation that coalesces individual spiritual longing with humanitarian love in a way that enables and empowers both to result in enlightenment that becomes evolution.

And then, starting with Dallas Willard's two forward paragraphs in Ruth Haley Barton's *Invitation to Solitude and Silence,* I encounter a vast chasm—a reality that cannot be put into words!

> I ended my day's reading with Hebrews: "So then, a sabbath rest still remains for the people of God; for those who enter God's rest also cease from their labors as God did from his. Let us therefore make every effort to enter that rest, so that no one may fall through such disobedience as theirs." Hebrews 4:9-11 RSV

I took a longer, new walk this afternoon up a long road behind the cabin property. I ended up at a cabin site. Not the Lodge, but with a footpath along the lakeshore, much shorter, that took me right back to my camper. I welcomed the shortcut. I love walking in the woods. My stamina and balance aren't what they once were, so I tire easily and struggle with a cane over the very uneven forest floor. I read well into the night.

≈ ≈ ≈

I awakened to a light drizzle. Dawn is just barely beginning. I got up, read for a while, and gleaned some great inspiration. After I ate breakfast, I went for a walk, but it was still raining and 65 degrees overnight and a 72-degree high today. I have limited clothing, no dryer, no clothesline, and the humidity is high enough that I must keep anything away from dampness in or under plastic boxes, including all my books. I stuff them in a bag when I finish reading at night. This is the first day it has been clear enough for a sunset, albeit behind a bank of forest.

I enjoyed two delightful walks today—40 minutes in the morning and over an hour in the afternoon. I'm getting stronger as I slowly recover from months of inactivity. On my first day here, 10-15 minutes was my limit. I managed these longer walks just fine today. Hoping to get to longer and longer walking soon.

My reading and study reflections have been exceptionally rich today. Many new and deep insights into truths I have never seen. I'm writing a good portion of them to keep them fresh and alive in my mind—and making writing them a habit.

I met a man who owns a camp about a mile from here where he caught a 25-pound rainbow trout off a bridge near my camper. I've seen some nice ones when I am walking each day, but I have no idea how to estimate their weight.

≈ ≈ ≈

So, how do I get "into the zone" that prompts these rich insights? I've been asked that question many times and promised to study my process and explain it. Today I wrote it down on my yellow pad and settled in to analyze it.

The bottom line, long story short: I sit down, tune into "Sparky" (my name for God's Holy Spirit, my observer, guide, and director of divine impulses), and then I follow whatever impulse I have. As I think, meditate, and pray, I write any insights that come to me. Then I read, write a little more, meditate more, perhaps for hours. I may read one sentence, one paragraph, and meditate at length to encourage these exciting ideas to arise from deep inside me.

The stillness here—the silence and peace in these woods—is deafening. When I choose to listen, which is more and more often these days, my mind grows full of great insights and inspiration. It's an adjustment, tuning into the silence in creative ways. It differs significantly from the sporadic silence we may find in the city. This is day and night, 24/7 silence, and I feel totally alone with my thoughts and God's faint whispers. I'm not used to this. It is not comfortable.

~ ~ ~

I had been up here only a few days when God smacked me on the side of the head and shouted boldly and loudly, "Larry! You fool! Why did you pay all that money to ship six boxes of books to study about the Source of life, when I brought you up here to live WITH the source of life—at your fingertips and in every breath?"

Well, I got the message to spend less time in books and practice the unknown, unfamiliar art of my being! Not DOING, which I have done my entire life. You see, I was taught that my worth and value were in what I did. God is helping me to see the standard equipment he birthed me with is my worth in who I AM—my BEING. Not what I do. I wish I had learned this lesson, as I am learning it in this Maine wilderness, much, much earlier in my life.

Humbly recognizing my naïveté, I boxed up all but a few of the books I brought with me to send home whenever I had the opportunity. Then I took my yellow pads, began building a pit fire each day and sitting in silence to listen, meditate, and write whatever came to me. I wrote over 400 pages of inspirations and insights I received from the sights and sounds, mystery and uncertainty, wonder and beauty of "our Father's world." I had experienced nothing like this before.

CHAPTER 4

Sunrise on Nicatous Lake

This early morning, sitting quietly and watching the morning unfold, random inspiring and insightful thoughts floating around my consciousness, I heard a familiar noise . . .

Was it a troop plane, arriving or departing from war? (Most of these planes stop at Bangor, 80 miles southwest of me, to refuel.) My temporary home lies in the flight path of planes carrying troops to and from war.

Was it a motorboat, bringing a family in from one of the islands? (It's the only way to get to and from this cabin.) On this 20-mile-long lake, many people live and vacation on its islands. The only access for them is by water, so boats are always coming and going to these homes.

Was it an ATV? Countless all-terrain vehicles pass by me daily, about a block from my camper. Many people up here enjoying the wilderness are on the way to one of the three fresh springs where everyone goes for water. (Yesterday a guy riding an ATV brought me water from a spring about five miles away.)

Was it a lumber truck, going or returning from a deposit of 100 tons of logs for the mill? The paper mill at Lincoln, 27 miles from here, makes most of the toilet paper for the nation. After they cut the tree, they trim all the branches off and then put it in a shredder. They then blow the shredded tree into a huge, 18-wheeled, low-bellied truck similar to a moving van. This truckload is then hauled out to make TP—and some of it is turned into particle board for Home Depot and Lowes.

Foresting is really mechanized these days. Everything from cutting trees to rolling them into smooth logs is done by a one-man operation on a huge, $600,000 saw and trimmer. The huge flat-bed 18-wheelers, sometimes with a trailer behind them the size of another 18-wheel truck bed, are called *porcupines*. The sides on the flat beds are steel posts six to eight feet high, positioned every four to six feet along the sides of the bed. I see empty porcupines go by and return, loaded, in about 30 minutes. What kind of equipment does this loading? No tie downs. Just 100 tons of long, straight logs.

Back to my noise. I could not tell the source until it got close enough to hear or see and identify it. In this case, it was three of the above four sources, getting to my sight and hearing nearly simultaneously. There was harmony and unity to the sound. I thought of the chairs in an orchestra. This variety of sounds in such close harmony was difficult for me, for a while, to distinguish what it was.

Does this say something about the harmony in much of God's world? Is it not possible for all 6.8 billion of our family of humans to move closer to unity and harmony as we all get closer to our common source?

I trust it is possible, and I choose to live my life in a way to invite this to happen by what I think (no judgment), what I feel (peace and harmony), what I say (serving love to every person as I am anointed to serve), and without judgment or criticism.

By making my actions congruent with Christ's love, I grow. This is a huge mission I shall do imperfectly as long as I live and strive to move closer and closer to this ideal. (John Wesley's "Going on to Perfection.")

There is a massive river of unconditional love to and through every one of the 6.8 billion in our family. May we be open to it and facilitate its coming!

~ ~ ~

This morning after I drank my coffee, read, wrote, meditated, thought, and had a wonderful, peaceful, quiet time, I took a two-plus mile walk, exploring unfamiliar territory. I found two rustic, reliable walking sticks—sturdy sticks help me balance, give my upper body more work out while walking, and it also strengthens my shoulders and arms.

I decided to take a swim to shower and shampoo in the lake. Water here has only been thawed for about two months, but it was not nearly as cold as I expected. It felt great to prepare me for my evening activities before bed.

I met a friendly couple from Florida on 4-wheelers today—we had a long visit. They have a camp in the southern part of Nicatous Lake, and they spend their summers here and winters in Florida. He's a retired Air Force helicopter pilot, 37 years in the service.

"Life is good!" he said.

"Even in war?" I countered.

He thought for a moment and then responded, "I have been in some nasty situations, but for the most part I chose to make it good, wherever I was and whatever I was doing."

~ ~ ~

At Sparky's urging today, I relaxed, moved a little more slowly. Learning to listen—really listen—to the whispers of the Holy Spirit is more of a challenge than I imagined. So deeply ingrained are the habits and rituals we tend to live by, it's so easy for the ego to override those faint nudges.

I've watched a hummingbird since daylight, darting in for a few sips of nectar at a time from my feeder. He returns every 10 or 15 minutes for more. Mid-morning, my little bird friend landed on my feeder, and we had a pleasant conversation. It looked at me between drinks as if to pause and say, "I'm having a delightful day being here—free, limitless, exploring, and curiously enjoying our new relationship."

What real awareness does this little bird have of me, of our connection in these woods? I know not! I am thrilled, inspired, and certain that these are sacred moments, just us. I found several nice places to just sit in the stillness and beauty and drink it in. I was relaxed; I didn't want to do anything but sit and be. This is an excellent exercise for me, busy, busy, busy as I have been all my life.

Today I also finally settled in for a phenomenal study time with insights bombarding me almost faster than I could record them in my journal. After sitting still for so long, I needed to move, so I went out for an afternoon stroll up a long dirt road where lots of ripe raspberries and blackberries remained, even after the bears had enjoyed their fill. This is really the backwoods—nothing but trees, mountains, and water everywhere you look. I ended my trek at "Unnamed Lake," pristine, native, and perfect. I sat in pure awe of the clear blue water, waves splashing upon sandy shores, and tall green forest all around! It was about a two-and-a-half-hour walk, a little over half of which was easy walking on the dirt road; the rest was slow, deliberate travel in the forest over very soft, uneven terrain with tons of needles and leaves carpeting the ground. I found it much, much more interesting walking with flowers, birds, and forest growth. My walking stick kept me stabilized. I'd never have made it through those woods without it.

Appreciating how my walking sticks help me stay stable, I stay on the lookout for good ones. (My walking sticks break eventually because most have been decomposing.) I found a good one on today's walk and spent the evening whittling on it. "It must be off of a maple tree," I thought, noticing that the wood was so hard my very sharp knife could hardly cut it. It had a lot of small branches that had broken off, but my knife wouldn't cut the nubbins. I finally found another hard stick and hammered these down as far as I could, then finished them off with my knife. They are sharp enough to cut my hands if I'm not very careful, so I want them off my cane!

It rained all night, some quite heavy, so I got up in the middle of the night to zip up all screens to keep water out. It is great sleeping with raindrops falling on my roof above me, three feet away.

I have water and supplies to last another week or more. I'll be fine without people checking in on me and providing food or water for a while. If I must go to "Plan B," I have met a few acquaintances here I know would help me.

CHAPTER 5

Island on Nicatous Lake

"**W**hy are you here?" he asked me casually as we ate.

"To see if I can find God!" I replied.

This set him back for an instant. Then he said with deep, moving conviction, looking up into the giant fir trees that canopied his house, "Well, you have come to the right place."

My thoughts return often to this first encounter with Jack and Jaime, a young couple from Massachusetts who soon became very good new friends. I met them my first week here, when I decided to stop in at their new home in the woods to escape an afternoon downpour—the hardest rain I've seen since I got here.

They both laughed heartily when they saw me and beckoned me inside. "That is standard fare up here," Jack said. "It does rain often, usually not hard, and it keeps things a sumptuous green, with flowers. Most of the flowers are gone by now. Springtime in the woods is loaded with a vast variety of flowers."

In the course of conversation, I mentioned the ironic challenge of getting water from the springs every day. They said they would be more than glad to get me water any time I need it. They offered that if I'd bring my five seven-gallon jugs one and a half miles to their house, whenever they went to get water on the ATV, they'd fill them and deliver them to my front door!

It's such a comfort to know that there are people up here who would be glad to help me if I need it, and I'm finding a genuine spirit of generosity, mostly. It is tough surviving up here—and people like Jack and Jaime seem to be indicative of the spirit of community in these woods.

Besides shelter from the continuing downpour, they offered me gracious hospitality in the form of a cup of coffee immediately, and then some bacon and home fries as Jack informed me he was considered by many to be "the best chef in Massachusetts."

I soon discovered that this self-introduction was no brag. He *is* a chef! Jack went on to say that he serves meals on request from any vacationer or natives. (He has 15 coming in for breakfast on Saturday.) Jaime is a nurse at a nursing home in Lincoln, 27 miles away; the closest town with supplies. She offered to buy supplies for me any time I need them. They are very hospitable and are proving to be my lifeline out here.

Their beautiful home was the culmination of a two-year project, just completed this summer, they said, and now they're going to live here year round. Jack told me how neighbors up here love and help neighbors as family. Every stranger (including me and anyone else who happens by) is invited into the fellowship. A pristine, pure, unmolested natural setting surrounded by forest, water, and a few great friends. Just this spring, he offered as example, their neighbors all came together to help put a new metal roof on their house. The reward? A prime rib dinner with all the trimmings from a prize-winning Boston chef!

~ ~ ~

Back in my camper, my thoughts bounced from my heritage in church then back to Jack and Jamie. They have no church and probably were never baptized. When I talked about searching for God, he replied with a peaceful, cheerful smile, "I don't know much about that. I just know I would rather be here than anyplace else in the world. Away from the rat race in Massachusetts."

He told me that living up here, only a few miles from Caribou, Maine, the coldest spot in the US in winter, taking care of one another isn't just a nicety. It's a mutual necessity—a matter of survival. "It gets 20-30 degrees below zero," he adds, "with snow-covered landscape for weeks and months. The snow is often deep, and it is 27 miles from gas, food, and the other necessities of life."

He shrugged. "There is peace and quiet beauty here," he said. "What few people who are brave enough to live here year round take care of each other. Where else do people take care of each other like we do up here?"

As I continued to ponder Jack's comment about how neighbors love and help neighbors as family, more and more depth to this seemingly happenstance meeting, conversation, and exchange of ideas emerged. Isn't this what life is all about? A warm, wholesome relationship with people and the natural world environment!?

Continuing to reflect on these deeper layers of this rich exchange with Jack and Jaime, a new and interesting question emerged:

How essential, then, is the church?

Jack and Jaime have no church background; they hardly know what I am talking about. They seem to live from within what I'd call Christian hospitality: compassion, caring, service to others. Did they come to this state of being via training from some source—or the intuitive awareness with which we were all born?

I'm inclined to think it is the latter. If we are all born into inner wisdom, the "I" of Christ, and society doesn't educate us out of our God-given sense of BEING, could they not come to this intuitively? Earlier civilizations, cultures, and tribes have (i.e., the Kalahari and Native American—and probably all native cultures, Taoism, Buddhism, etc.).

On the plus side, my observation says:

- the values I cherish as a Christian are taught and reinforced repeatedly, nurtured, and healed by the church community;

- corporately, we can do so much more in the ministry of caring, loving truth through the church (i.e., hospitality, school, ministries of compassion, etc.), and challenging unhealthy forces in society. However, we need new strategies here.

- the church can build powerful families, marital models for living (as other institutions also can).

On the negative side, I see:

- ❧ we are so controlled by the need for money and survival that in many respects we have lost our proper mission;

- ❧ we wait to be instructed by our Source in each decision we make;

- ❧ we forget to live in the Present, *now* moment to be directed by the Holy Spirit, which pushes us to be motivated more by "How can I serve?" than "How can I be Christ's actual presence in the world?"

- ❧ we struggle to let go of individuality and tribal instincts, and accept in love and compassion for every person as brothers and sisters—family—to model Christian hospitality and caring in ways that make others say, "I want that!"

This requires practicing daily habits. Not from rote, "ought to," and habits, but by living into the question each day: "What do I need to do this day to *be* Christ's love in the world—and what holy habit and law, what style, will help me most to get there?"

God has gifted each of us with unique ways in which to serve our world. I have a unique, custom-fit practice of holy habits to condition and direct me spontaneously in my moment-to-moment life. We must practice being guided by this inner wisdom, the "I" of Christ, rather than any external person, model, book, or program that says, "Do it this way!"

~ ~ ~

My encounter with Jack and Jaime—and my subsequent pondering and meditations have prompted some deep, penetrating questions:

For a wholesome, healthy life, living in relationship to my Source do I need a degree in theology?

Do I need Baptism and Communion?

Do I need membership in a church for a wholesome life?

Do I need a certain set of religious beliefs from the Bible?

Do I need what the church and others say are essential? Do I need to know the Bible?

Bottom line: is not the essence of a holy, healthy life found in quality relationships with my neighbor? Is it not a wholesome, holy relationship to my environment—the sanctuary of my Source, where God lives—that is found in people and not things?

Do I have something Jack and Jaime don't have—and vice versa? Open questions to ponder more deeply!

CHAPTER 6

In my early morning meditation times, I feasted on *Sounds of the Eternal: A Celtic Psalter* by John Philip Newell . Today, with the sun slowly rising, the colors of the misty predawn sky reflecting the ambiance of each moment, changing as clouds come and go. As the sun rose, the sky became a brilliant red, then too soon turned pink, and shortly thereafter, a soft, gray sky.

Last night's gentle rain left the air a fresh-but-humid 68 degrees. I took my shirt off. Leaning back into the screen of one of my windows, I felt a drop of water splash my forehead, then my chest. The giant fir tree, standing at least 60 feet or more above me, had quietly baptized me in its silent might. I gazed up at this enormous tree that had weathered every storm of the past decades. Despite the elements of its surroundings—wind, blizzards, 30 feet of snow, lightning—it stood mighty, strong, tall, tenacious, and courageous.

I took a deep breath and let this awareness settle within me. What more can I add?

Upon reflection, I realized I am baptized every moment of every day with incredible power, endurance, peace, love, and compassion—from more sources than I have ever yet recognized."

Awaken! Be aware! Celebrate!

~ ~ ~

Creature comforts—you never know what you might find in the woods.

It's been a low energy day of reading, study, and a long stretch of time spent watching the traffic at the busy dock across the way. I wrote a bit more, ate some lunch, then set out for an afternoon walk that proved delightful—and I encountered three fresh moose tracks crossing the road.

As I continued on, I discovered another surprise, somewhat less organic but nevertheless surprising and delightful in a different way. At a small campsite I like to visit from time to time I noticed a path from its clearing I had not seen before. After a 200-yard walk up this path out of the clearing I spotted a square frame with hardware cloth on all four sides and a nice seat on top—a ready-made open toilet with a commercial seat! There was even an old bed sheet hanging on a nearby limb for privacy!

Arriving back at camp, energized by my walk, the fresh air, and my delighted discoveries, I found that someone had delivered some coffee from town, which was a great blessing because I had only one day's worth left. On the way back I stopped for a chat with Lisa, who owns this camp, and at her request I gave her my card with Patty and the kids' numbers on it in case of an emergency. These unexpected kindnesses are gifts for this ol' geezer in the woods! She, too, accommodates me to grocery shop or get water when it's needed, and she's here until September 1. Nice to have a couple of backup plans!

~ ~ ~

I woke up excited to see evidence of the approaching dawn reflecting off the surface of the lake. A chilly 62 degrees—down from 80 yesterday when I went shirtless most of the day—prompted me to get a fire going while I waited for the sun to warm me.

Then I realized nature's trickery. The light I saw on the lake was actually a reflection of a sliver of moonlight in the Eastern sky. Stars still brilliantly twinkling in the east, overhead, and in the west lay out a scene of magnificence and wonder overhead! "Oh, Lord, how magnificent is thy work in all the earth!" I whispered aloud in the sheer awe of that sacred moment.

Without a timepiece to confirm my suspicion, I discerned I must have awakened about 2:00 a.m. when, after sitting in this spectacular nighttime stillness for at least two hours (very glad for the fire keeping me warm), that daylight was beginning to break on the east horizon. Feeling blessed by God's subtle sense of humor, I got a pad and pencil and started my day's writing. Fresh new thoughts and inspirations were flooding my whole being, almost faster than I could capture them in writing.

I thought about this new paradox of light I had just witnessed. The gospels invite us to get out there and let our light shine. "Don't hide your light under a basket," Jesus said. But out here in the middle of the night, in total darkness, I got in touch with such wonder, grandeur, and bliss I do not know how to put it into words. It was breathtaking!

I thought, "I might just get transported to an even better world, right here, right now! What a beautiful worship experience!"

Then God poked me in the ribs. "You like this, Larry?"

"I sure do, God, Most Holy One!"

"Well, let me tell you a secret. There is a lot of darkness back in the world you left behind. When you take time to get still and listen, *this* is the majesty and wonder of human needs I want addressed! You need to get back into that world and let your light shine!"

My friend Byron has a mantra he lives with all day long, day after day: "God's Light, God's light, God's healing light!" That mantra has helped him heal from two serious bouts with the life-threatening disease of cancer.

Oh! How I want to hear that and live that! I want to hear it loud and clear in my ear, every day. "Go out and be God's people in the world" every day. That light, God's light, heals bodies and heals society.

And one more thing. When you're sitting by a campfire as close as possible to stay warm and listen for a fresh new word from the very source of your life, stay out of the smoke! That's both humor *and* dead serious!

After the colors of dawn had faded into a misty grey, I realized I was hungry, so I fixed a hot oatmeal breakfast with a fresh pot of coffee. Out of curiosity, I re-read my instructions for making coffee on the can. What do you know! I realized I'd been using 2 or 3 times more coffee than necessary. I knew the taste wasn't right but didn't know why. And, with my sweetener supply depleted, drinking such extra-strong coffee without it was an adventure.

Good thing I know how to laugh!

And speaking of laughing, do you know how to make God laugh? I learned in Maine.

I spent all kinds of money to ship six boxes of books here ahead of me. I told myself that with three months of uninterrupted study time I would think I had died and gone to heaven! At home there's never enough time to read all the things I want to read, or to spend the time with readings I really want to savor. What better place than this to indulge that lifetime longing?

Oh, fool that I am. What is the value of a book when you are living in a natural sanctuary, where it is impossible to look anywhere and *not* see, hear, and taste a noble word from the very source of the fountain of life? I went to Maine to learn to be. Isn't there something ironic about taking a library with me to the woods to do that?

And God chuckled!

CHAPTER 7

Sunrise and fog on Nicatous Lake

awakened this morning from a most frustrating dream. Half awake, at first I thought I had missed the dawn, then I felt the rush of gratitude as I realized that was also part of the dream. I climbed out of bed feeling disoriented. In my hurry to get outside, I ran into my kitchen bench, knocking things to the floor.

So eager to repeat the scene from a few nights before, I was relieved to encounter that star-lit blanket as still my only view to the east, west, and above me! I had no idea what time it was. After building my fire, I waited two hours to see my dawn. As I waited, enjoying my fire and my properly measured coffee, I journaled my dream.

In this dream, my frustration was building to a crescendo as I was supposed to move out of my apartment or dorm room on this particular day. As the day progressed, remodelers came in, framed the doors and windows with sheetrock, and plastered their seams into a smooth wall.

I had friendly conversations with the workers—calm, joking, having fun, no hurry. Then I came in a bit later to find that my room, doors, and windows had all gotten the same treatment.

Alarmed, I asked for the foreman, who was upstairs. He kindly came down, laughing and joking, friendly as could be, though I had not seen him before.

I was explaining my problem, exasperated and angry at this point, and this is when I awakened, full of different feelings—frustration, anger, fear, and relief that, "Whoa! This is thankfully only a dream!" I was really fired up!

Thus, the crazy, seeing-what-was-not-true and coming out of bed awkward and kicking.

In his book, *Dreams: God's Forgotten Language*, John Sanford draws on C.G. Jung's work to reveal the psychological and spiritual significance of dreams to help us find healing and wholeness and reconnect us to a living spiritual world. I use this book to work on some of my more intriguing and complex dreams, certain there are messages there to unpack that could be helpful to me. Thoughts I've processed about the meaning of this dream:

- I am in a very intense process of finding new ways to think, feel, live, and serve.
- "Apartment"—old beliefs I'm dropping, preparing for something new! Remodeling!
- Friendly foreman and workers—each are me, having a blast in my process.
- Frustration and anger—the ego part of me, kicking and screaming and saying, "I will have no part of this losing of power and control over my life."

After working through the dream, I was awash in relief and joy that I am on the right course, even though I may question it at times.

~ ~ ~

Is God a what or a who? It's an important debate, I think. I believe the answer we each ultimately come to is going to have a very profound effect on the quality of life we live!

This debate still reverberating within me, I stood on the lake shore watching a new family of ducks. It appeared Mama released her kiddos to go anywhere on the lake. I couldn't see Mama with the other four ducklings. Either they were off their home base and headed out across the lake, or Mama was in charge of an exercise in independence.

Watching the ducks, I stood there soaking up the wonderful heat from the sun, trying to get warm. My fire nearly went out. I created my very own psalm of praise! Thankful for the warm, caring, compassionate, low lighting, and the peaceful, silent, sacred sanctuary.

With all its natural appointments, objects to enhance my worship experience, I was grateful for the peace of the setting; the peace I experienced probably more profoundly and deeply than at any time in my life since birth. (And I am not sure how peaceful that was—before birth, probably very peaceful. After birth I probably started my stress conditioning almost immediately.)

~ ~ ~

The deeper I explore the ground of my being, the higher my antenna goes to pick up new messages from the universe—messages I never heard in the same way before. Consider the clear, resonant song of the loon—unique and haunting—with never any doubt where that sound is coming from. The higher my antenna, the more that song sends shivers up my spine.

How did Patty know in January where we would live in May? (United Methodist preachers get notified of any transfers each May.) Her antenna was a whole lot higher than mine. We all have this capacity. Some have more highly developed versions than others.

It is called intuition, hunches, gut feelings, or Divine messages. "Divine bullets that are flying by us constantly, faster than machine gun fire." The higher my antenna, the more bullets hit it. It is also called the Holy Spirit—God with us in every breath!

This morning the loons have been unusually verbal and melodious! I'd hear loons nearby me on the north start their communication chorus. Then I would hear antiphonal loons on my near south.

My, what conversations they have sometimes and how it thrills the soul to sit in silence and absorb the song. This, for me, was one of the greatest gifts of the wilderness!

CHAPTER 8

Magnificent dawn

've spent a lot of time lately watching the comings and goings of my neighbor. Over time, I've observed the increase in curiosity that eventually led him to cross the ravine that separated us and, after several false starts, second thoughts and retreats, take a bold leap—right onto my utility table "cupboard" to check out the two full coffee cans of reserve birdseed.

After watching him pry open one of the cans, and then eat to his heart's content, I spent a good portion of the day today observing my neighbor (Frisky, as I named this determined little ground squirrel) filling his cheeks with birdseed and then darting away to stash it in his home for the winter.

Between yesterday's long walk and Frisky's relentless expenditure of energy, I needed a recuperative nap. A cool, 65-degree breeze surrounded me as I drifted off to sleep, and I slept deeply until I gradually became aware of the unmistakable sound of children playing in the distance. Groggy but refreshed, I drank some water and made my way to the door of my camper where I was able to see the dock across the inlet. I watched families of all sizes come and go from that dock regularly, and today there must have been 15 kids playing there, all ages, laughing and enjoying their afternoon with their families.

That water must have been cold—but it didn't seem to bother them! Lots of laughing, squealing, games, and general great fun. These New Englander kids grow up together in these camps every summer. What a gift! What a heritage!

~ ~ ~

As I fixed myself a sandwich, ideas continued to bubble up. I went back to my yellow tablet and wrote like crazy until midafternoon. Then, needing to stretch my legs a bit, I walked to Jack and Jaime's place to ask for help getting water on their next trip to the spring. After a nice visit I returned to my home in the woods for more silence and writing.

I picked up Richard Rohr's *The Naked Now* writings and found myself transfixed with his ideas. He's spot on in how the Western big three religions focus on the rational only to neglect the mystical. They have truly shot themselves in the foot. Rohr offers profoundly simple ways to correct this. His proposed solution is the biggest challenge anyone will ever have. It is a challenge, in my opinion, that is necessary if Christianity is to survive as a transforming force in America.

After a delicious supper of bean-and-bacon soup, I did my chores and zipped up for another cold night. I read a book for a while and then retired. Another unique and wonderful day learning how to be silent and listen!

~ ~ ~

Ask and ye shall receive. My recent study of Sanford's dream book helped me set my intention to study it more deeply to see what else this work might yield. So, when I asked for a dream, I got a clear, detailed one at 3:00 a.m. At first I did not want to get up in the 42-degree night air to work the dream or even record it.

But just about the time I made the decision to go back to sleep and record the details later, I realized I was too awake to not get on with it, so I got up, made some coffee, and recorded my dream.

My efforts were rewarded with magnificent dawn, and after I finished the dream work I sat in silence to drink in the infinite changing scenes, colors, light and clouds. I knew I was observing The Master Artist at work, and I was inspired, filled with wonder, and nearly overwhelmed by the creative ideas flowing through me. I grabbed a handful of dried fruit and went into my creative mode until mid-morning, when pangs of hunger led me to cook myself a bowl of hot oats.

I enjoyed some great reading time the rest of the morning, followed by lunch and a good nap. And then, because I'd been so sedentary all day, I went out for my longest walk yet, all the way to the West Lake Camp site. I took the North Westlake Road two miles to a near dead end. Along the way, I saw some neat, creative cabin sites—48 of them in all.

On the way back I met a nice Mainer named Mitford, and we had a great visit. Exhausted when I got back to camp, I was also exhilarated by my long, beautiful walk in the perfect 68 degrees with a light breeze. I ate, read for a while, and then retired pooped!

~ ~ ~

I learned today that there is a two-week limit on all Maine public campsites, so I have two weeks to move or get admonished by the forestry service. My camping spot on Porter Cove is only big enough for one camper. It is a neat, neat, private spot. I really hated the very idea of leaving it.

I appealed to Chris, the Forest Ranger, and shared my dilemma: I needed to be here five more weeks. I had nowhere else to go—and this late in the season it was doubtful that anyone would want this site.

To my great relief, he said he'd cover for me and allow me to stay here for the remainder of my time in Maine. Hooray!

Then a different ranger appeared the next day with some scary news. There was a forest fire located about a quarter mile from me, and he was there to investigate, trying to pinpoint the source.

He eyed me—and my campsite—suspiciously.

"Did you cause the fire?" the ranger probed. "Did you see or hear anyone who might have caused it?"

I assured him how careful I was was with my fires. "I *never* leave it unattended," I said. "I *always* douse it before bedtime, AND," I said, gesturing to the two full buckets of lake water at the edge of my site, "I *always* keep a couple of large buckets of lake water nearby to douse any stray sparks."

He peered at me, silent for a moment, and then seemingly satisfied I was telling the truth, moved his investigation on to the next campsite.

I contemplated both encounters well into the night—and how they illustrated the contrast between *ego self* and *authentic self*—well into the night. Was it my ego self, working hard to impress the ranger who came to inspect my fire trustworthiness? Was it my authentic self who appealed, "I need to stay another five weeks" to the first ranger? Neither was bad or wrong, but my belief is that when I am in my ego self, I respond one way. When I am in my authentic self I respond very differently.

How do I know which part of me is speaking? I believe this is a very pertinent question that we alone must learn to interpret. I believe the more I live in my authentic self, the more my ego self withers away. So, it becomes clearer and easier to choose. With my authentic self, the newer I am in this process, the foggier my eyes are to see and the denser my ears are to hear. My ego easily and subtly tricks me to go with my ego self. My long history and practice here can keep me in the fog.

Reflecting on how I follow God and Spirit, I sit quietly and thoughtfully consider each option through the lens of *being* versus *doing* . As I mentally rehearse each option, asking "is this being?" ("yes" or "no"), Or doing? ("yes" or "no"), I usually get one clear "yes." Sometimes far more yeses with doing, which is often *my* choice.

Another litmus test often can be asking, "Which decision benefits more people?" And "which one could bring negative consequences?" This sharpens my answer many times.

~ ~ ~

A lot of people are familiar with the expression, "Let go and let God."

I think there are two ways to do this.

The first is passive: "I'm helpless, God, you do it for me." This approach works for some, who then say that "God's will" is the reason for anything that happens, good or bad: "It's a God thing."

This is something I don't believe. I think *I* create the "good" and the "bad" in my life. I think whether an outcome is "good" or "bad" is subjective, and God doesn't make those valuations. We do. So I ask, "Is that God or is that me?" This is part of my darkness to explore.

The second is more complicated and requires a sense of personal responsibility for your life: "God, be my guide!" When I am living out of this, I'll take the responsibility for my decisions and their outcome, "good" or "bad," knowing that God is always there to guide me quietly and anonymously.

And when we say, "God be my guide," does this also include asking for Divine guidance from people who have crossed over, people who are there guiding us all the time? Does it matter whether God is guiding me or someone who has crossed over is guiding me? Is there really any difference?

It's 3:30 a.m., so I look to the east to see if dawn was beginning to break—with my bright headlight shining above my head!

O, Lord! How often have I looked for Your light and guidance—and then crowded it out with my own, selfish, ego-centered light?

Then God enlightened me. "Larry? "Turn off *your* light! *My* flashlight works just fine!"

~ ~ ~

After my discussion with the suspicious ranger, I began contemplating my style of fire building—and then considered it metaphorically.

I start with tinder, dry pine, pinecones, pine needles, then small twigs, bigger and bigger wood, sized 1-2 inches. Then, I place a cedar or maple log or limb on top. My architecture is a tipi—style with 1-2 sticks around it and light the fire, adding to it whenever I choose.

Is this a metaphor about how to build a life?

Each morning, I become a more exquisite fire builder. This is life for me! The older and more experienced I get, the better I get! Frequently, the kid in me starts arranging the fire how I think best, and I make it worse. Nature knows best!

This is my agenda for living forward—nature knows best.

~ ~ ~

We often don't see our own selfishness. We can't see our own controlling. So, it's important to ask the part of you that knows and understands these things the following questions—and then be still enough to hear the answers arising from within your own being:

- How am I selfish?
- How am I controlling?
- What are my challenges?
- What are my opportunities?
- Where are my infinite possibilities?
- What has shaped my life of spiritual formation?

Having the patience to ask these questions and explore the answers is part of my challenge. Just like my encounter with the rangers, it's not that black and white, and it's up to us to discover how we create our own conscious choices and experiences.

(HAPTER 9

My go-to spot for quiet inspiration.

I n sitting by the fire, tending the flames, observing the nuances of different fires on different days, I found a new sanctuary. It was this sacred space of deep contemplation and connection that brought me to the fire pit day after day for fresh observation, new insight, and, more often than not, new light on old beliefs and habits and attitudes. This was at once humbling and inspirational. I will attempt to share a core group of these fireside insights in this chapter, and then return to the fire pit from time to time as this story and its associated metaphors continue to unfold.

I burned a lot of wood during my three months in Maine. I had a fire going each morning from 2:00 or 3:00 a.m. until I went to bed each evening, between 7:00 and 9:00 p.m. Much of this wood I gathered from the nearby woods. A decent supply was stacked about a mile away from my camp but had to be carried that distance over some uneven and rugged terrain. The focus of much of my typical day, therefore, was gathering wood.

In learning the difference between types of wood, how it burned, how to arrange the different wood varieties for the best result, I uncovered parallel after parallel with my own life, my life in the church, and the faith community as a whole. All of this consumed much of my thinking, imagination, and contemplation.

If I build it right, I can have a hot fire—starting with fresh hardwood, then placing the old, garbage wood on top. *Garbage wood* is older, softer, in stages of decay and returning to Mother Earth. It flames up a bit here and there, and it doesn't really burn until it drops into that hot, hot bed of coals created by the hardwood. These white-hot coals ultimately change the wood I add from particle to wave, from wood to gas, energy for rain, etc.

The old garbage roots I put on my fire bent into a U—curved, ugly, and old. Left alone, it melded into a bent, cohesive center that eventually, with a bit of shepherding, tending, layering, and nurturing, created a beautiful fire. Out of old and ugly comes beauty—good, blessing, cohesive unity, and power! This beauty and power all naturally moves toward the center, where the hottest heat (Christ) does what it's supposed to do (church).

Considering how this relates to work in the church, it takes that bed of white-hot coals to ignite dead wood—or even fresh, live wood—to burn for ministry and "being God's people in the world." How do we become that white-hot coal that ignites anything that touches it?

One hard, hard, slow lesson I've had to learn with fire is that I need to do a *lot* less shepherding, tending, layering, and nurturing. Sometimes it's better to just relax and let it do its natural thing! Do we sometimes do more harm than good in trying to be "in control" of family, of church?

~ ~ ~

I'm coming to see that perhaps some of my joy at playing with my morning fire is regression to my younger years when my friends and I would go down to the city dump and play for hours. We came up with new games, new toys, and new creations made from all manner of things we found in the endless supply of the dump.

I'm settling into the awareness that sometimes there is a metaphorical dump that can offer an endless supply of tools to help us in our lives! Which discarded ideas at our fingertips could help us in our lives, if only we take a moment to play with them? My morning fires are helping me to observe a good number of thoughts and ideas that would otherwise go unnoticed. Sitting here, giving myself the time to observe and listen, I feel an opening to new ideas.

Is truth so elusive, paradoxical and undefinable that I can only think or ponder it in metaphor? It seems to me these are the thoughts that point to God's truth. When I consider the many aspects of my morning fires I've observed and noted—stray sparks, what fuels different kinds of flames, the role of embers and oxygen—I see the many metaphors to consider for church work.

There are so many parallels between fire building and spirit building in our lives. If I crowd the logs too closely, they will burn, but not well. What does that say about a crowded schedule?

The logs need space around them to get oxygen to the fire. The more oxygen, the better it burns. We all need God's oxygen to keep our fire burning. How do we get God's oxygen?

Mulling over the theology tucked into all these fire metaphors, I open the door to more curiosity—how does wind fit into fire? In Hebrew scriptures the same word for wind, *ruach*, can be translated as "wind" or "breath," and refers more to power than essence. The stronger the wind, the hotter the fire. The more oxygen gets to the hot coals, the more they turn white-hot, the hottest wood gets. What is the lesson, the insight there for us? Why was my attention drawn to this thought?

One possibility I see has to do with conflict. Honest conflict, negotiated to resolution in restorative, reconciling, caring, listening ways, as Christ suggests and used (the "Third Way") calls for "fresh oxygen." These tools he shared with us are so very useful and helpful for building community and cohesiveness. Creating unity out of conflict fans the fire, increases the heat, and fuels our effectiveness.

~ ~ ~

I decided to settle in for a bit, just to contemplate the many important metaphors I'm finding around this fire.

The hot coals in my fires do far more for the fire than the little duty I do from time to time, trying to see a flame I think I want to see and enjoy. Does the invisible heat from the daily practice, practice, practice of living a new life in Christ do more for mission and ministry than the little flames we try to ignite?

I built some large fires, and I built some small, intimate fires that only had a flame or two. *Is one more vital? More important than the other?*

It is the hot individual coals that instantly ignite the new wood I put on the fire. Why do I enjoy watching the new flame more than the powerful, but more inconspicuous coals?

It is the mixture of both new, flaming wood and the invisible coals that truly make a fire. Aren't they both essential for keeping the fire alive?

Each of us is a burning coal. We ignite others by grace and love, and the flame joins us deeper in fellowship. Those we ignite then become the burning coals to ignite others. It all started with one match—Jesus!

Consider what this process of igniting others has meant—in schools, hospitals, seminary, clinics, individuals, and mission teams. The spread of love and compassion goes all over this world in ways we may have seen or know about, and in many ways we may not know about.

As I get near the end of my fire each day, I toss piles of dry twigs, leaves, and partial branches on the fire, and after a period of time this leads to quite a hot conflagration of my remnant fire. How is this a metaphor for growing the effectiveness of church in the world? For me, this is about helping to build a new church, a new cell group, and/or new study groups. These new pieces of wood then become the very coals that ignite new fires in the life of the church and its community.

By using large hardwood, maple, or cedar, my fire burns slowly, creating hot, hot coals. I can keep this kind of fire burning until I'm ready to quit for the day, when I extinguish it with water. Each previous day's fire becomes the foundation for starting my new fire the next day. Within the context of our lives, our relationships build these kinds of sustainable fires within. Caring for these relationships continues to fuel the fire for a period of time, but as time passes, and perhaps the care of the relationship wanes, those fires can dwindle and even perhaps die.

I love cedar in my fire. Aside from burning well, it cracks and sparks and smells delicious. I love the smell of burning cedar. The downside to cedar is how those sparks can jump—and sometimes into my wood supply and start another fire. Sometimes the sparks hit my bare legs or burn holes in my clothes, which can burn Larry unless addressed quickly! (That's precisely how I learned to keep water handy, as I assured the young ranger.)

No matter how beautiful and delightful our life is, there are always sparks jumping out at us. When we think or react too quickly with immediate fear or anger, is this how holes get burned in our relationships? And what about unconditional love? How does unconditional love fit into the journey of sparks, whether contained or rogue?

I must decide and determine what I want to put into action or inaction. How do I want to respond when "sparked," and what are my feelings about it? When I criticize, judge, or discount the other person, that doesn't fit into my program as I envision it.

Thank you, God, for another wonderful awareness to help me learn, prepare adequately, and ready myself for the next spark—which is sure to come!

Here's another fire fact I learned the hard way—and the rich field of metaphor it offered me. Seasoned wood doesn't have to touch a coal to ignite—it can just be *nearby* to ignite new fuel and catch fire! We never know how the coals of our life touch someone and may ignite others—directly or indirectly. The hotter our coals, the more influence they have on others!

It is very common with the mega fires I build each day for a hot ember to fall off a log or branch and into a nest of wood chips and kindling that naturally gathers at an open pit fire. These red-hot embers could ignite a new fire—even a forest fire—but they don't! Why don't these fallen embers from my fire ignite another, auxiliary fire or even a forest fire?

Two metaphors I see here: first, I am always tending the fire to make sure that doesn't happen; and second, these embers need other hot coals to survive. What does that say to us? We need each other to keep the fire of Pentecost alive.

~ ~ ~

Sometimes my way is not the best way.

A further lesson arises from this fire thinking.

Every fire is unique and different. No matter how I plan to make it like a previous fire, ("it was my best one yet!"), every piece of wood is different. How it fits into the configuration of the fire is different. Thus, I must continually change my fire-building strategies, even as it burns.

As I play with and tend my fire, I arrange the wood my way, thinking it will enhance the fire. Well, there are times when my way won't work. Wood keeps rolling off. And then, when I give up, letting a log lay where it chooses to lay, it enhances the fire more than where I thought it ought to go. Is God's work with us a lot like that? Isn't that exactly how my Maine trip developed?

If I want my life to go the way I want it to go, I am required to expect and adjust to change. (Jesus said this!) I need or want to become more aware of whether I am trying to control my life to satisfy my own narcissistic, ego, or selfish ideals—or working out of unconditional love. What part of my life is my own doing, and what part is ignited by the spark of a silent, anonymous, bigger plan?

For me, each of the above are rich mysteries—not just theoretical, esoteric head stuff, but the very essence of life. As I seek to become less compulsive and controlling, I've become more committed to listening much more than talking.

Watching my fire, I see a tiny, dry twig that has turned red hot—and became a cinder beneath the larger branch that once gave it life. The heat of the small branch ignited its mother branch and set it on fire! (. . . "and a little child shall lead them.") Small, random acts of kindness can save lives and lead people to transformation. What unexpected futures have passed from one generation to another because of one little unsuspecting spark, flame, or hot coal?

God, I want to be one of those hot, hot coals that smolder and keep the blaze alive. This is my solid commitment. And it doesn't escape my notice that for the hot coal to stay alive to do its thing, it needs others around it to keep the heat, glow, and usefulness!

CHAPTER 10

My neatly managed fire.

When the large green personal vehicle came speeding into my campsite, red lights flashing, I was sitting in my lawn chair at the shore of the lake. It was some time in the middle of the afternoon. Jolted out of my lakeside reverie, I watched as the forest ranger jumped out of his vehicle and hurried toward me.

"Officer, what's up?" I said, rising from my chair to meet him.

"We have a forest fire in the area," he replied, stern and all-business. He walked past me to where my chair was perched, stood for a moment, surveyed my campsite and surrounding area, and then looked toward what I later learned was the area where the fire had started, less than a quarter mile from me. (I also later learned that his visit was prompted by his wondering, "Is this the idiot who started the fire?")

He didn't say another word.

I returned to my chair while he continued to stand nearby. In the distance, I heard a two-way radio conversation going on, then a call for the ranger, to which he responded in terse, clipped, one-word answers. He remained rooted in place for the duration of this exchange, just looking around my site.

Several more minutes passed without another word from him, and then he turned, walked back to his truck, lights still whirling, and remained in the cab for 20 minutes, scribbling on his clipboard.

I remained calm, continued my nature watch, and tried not to stare as he continued to write. In time, he put his vehicle in gear, paused, and slowly pulled away out of my camp, and on down the road.

My inquiring mind kept chattering, "What's going on? Why was he here? What was he looking for?"

Another thing I didn't know at the time (but later found out), was that there was a total fire ban in this forest because of the harsh, dry weather. The lake was down about two feet, and the entire woods around my camp was a tinderbox, a potential forest fire just waiting to happen.

And here I've been having huge pit fires from 2:00 to 3:00 a.m. until noon every day, enjoying every minute, blithely and innocently unaware.

Fortunately for me, when the ranger came to my camp my morning fire was long gone. I realized, however, that he was probably looking at the huge pile of old wood I had gathered to start my daily fires. It is illegal to cut any live wood in the forest, but gathering and burning dead and decayed wood is permitted—as long as there wasn't a burn ban.

I also later found out he was the area's head fire expert, stationed 50 miles from my camp, brought in to pinpoint the cause and response. Analyzing the whole situation now, my assumption is that the ranger rushed in to determine the cause, which he assumed was me (as I later learned) and to manage the fire at my site with the men in the field. Except there was no fire at my site and I was not the cause, which must have irritated him somewhat.

Shortly after the ranger left, the manager of the camp arrives in her stocking feet, having walked down the rocky road to my camp.

"I wanted to let you know there is a forest fire nearby," she said as she drew closer. "The forest service may want to use your campsite as a base from which to draw water for their trucks. You may have to evacuate. We have a room at the lodge that is yours with bed and bedding, and you can come on over anytime you need to."

She paused, looking down the three-quarter-mile path to the lodge from my camper, then added, "if they evacuate you, just tell the ranger you need a ride to the lodge, and we'll come and get you."

Now how about that for an "angels unawares" (Hebrews 13:2 KJV), offering such kind hospitality to a stranger? I have no transportation, no phone that works in this area of Maine, and no computer or radio to the outside world. And then she just shows up and offers essential aid to a guy who may really need her!

~ ~ ~

Thank goodness for Porter Point Camps!

The next crashing wave arrived a few hours later, just as the adrenaline from the earlier excitement had begun to subside. The person who loaned me the camper roared up in his SUV, oblivious to the fire and surrounding drama, and announced, "Larry, we will be here at 7:00 a.m. in the morning to move you. Here are some boxes. Get packed tonight to clear out the camper. I also need you to find someone to take down the pop-up camper and bring it to Burlington before Sunday so we can get it cleaned and ready for its new owner!"

Completely unrelated to the fire and evacuation for that reason, with his unexpected appearance I learned that the camper I was staying in had been for sale all summer, and he now had a buyer who was coming on Sunday to pick it up. It was already 4:00 p.m. How's that for an unexpected challenge?

"You'll need to find another place to live immediately," he said, as if that wasn't obvious and even perhaps impossible.

Remembering the camp manager's kind offer, I hoofed it the three quarters of a mile to Porter Camp to see if there was any possibility of an available cabin. (They stayed booked solid.)

"Anything will do," I implored after telling them my story. "If you even have a tent I can put up, I can make it work!"

As it turned out, the owners of Porter Camp had an empty log cabin, built in the 1890s out on the very end of the peninsula. "It's rustic," the manager said, "but the scenery is beautiful. It's the highest point on the property, with woods and water on three sides you can see from the cabin." She said that to the east, where the screened-in porch was, there was a clearing of the trees that offers a perfect view of both the lake and the forest beyond.

"It's a little leaky and I'm not sure what else you'll be getting into," she added, handing me the key. "We didn't rent that cabin this summer because it needed some major roofing repairs, but I think it will be adequate shelter for you—and you are welcome to use it for the rest of your time here."

It was not only adequate; it was *perfect* for me. A quarter mile from all the other cabins and sheltered from noise from the main camp. Silent and peaceful, with incredible views.

When God unfolds the plans, this is often how they go. All of this was happening, as if according to a perfect, pre-ordained plan. Was it? I really don't know.

I spent half the night packing my belongings into the boxes and bags to get out of the camper before 7:00 a.m. the next morning, and the kind camp manager sent a pickup to help me move to the 1890s cabin before the camper owners arrived. All the way around, this unbelievable turn of events was a dream solution if ever there was one!

The sequence of events surrounding my accommodations, the unfailing synchronicity of changes that worked together for my good—and keeping some kind of roof over my head throughout my stay—always makes me smile.

≈ ≈ ≈

The gifts of adversity.

Sitting on my screened-in porch on the east side of my cabin, the temperature has moved from 58 to 61 damp, cold degrees. The brisk, sometimes strong, wind is coming straight out of the east, right off the lake, hitting me in the face and exposed extremities. This breeze is so strong I had to shut my east kitchen window, just three feet from my stove, so my coffee would percolate.

Looking out at the spectacular view that surrounds me, I notice a small, new grove of Douglas Fir trees, 1-inch to 8-feet high, in the clearing between me and the lake. These little trees are whipping and bending in the wind to the point it looks like they would break—but they don't.

Those trees bend and whip now to build strength and endurance for the later days when they will be much taller, handling much stronger elements of wind, snow, and rain. They practice from infancy to be flexible, to go with the flow of external forces so that when these stressors come later in life, their experience teaches them to handle the stress and remain healthy and strong.

What an exquisite parallel to our lives and how our experiences prepare us for handling our own adversity.

~ ~ ~

I admit it. I've always had a profound prejudice against Christian worshipers who put their arms up in the air when they sing, pray, and/or worship.

And now that I find myself feeling so exhilarated at times in these woods, I get it! Every morning I put my arms up as high in the air as I can reach (it's good exercise, too!) and say, "Thank you! Thank you! Thank you, Creator, Sustainer, and Provider for 'leading me beside still waters' for three hours where 'my cup overflowed' day after day after day. I find this form of praise quite edifying!"

Now don't go telling anybody. My God! What would people back home think?

CHAPTER 11

Screened-in porch where Mr. Mouse and I came to an agreement

I'm considering the disconnect between how very wasteful I can be in my spending and frugality—one of John Wesley's cardinal themes. Over my lunch of hot beef ravioli with a container of green peas, suddenly I heard a noise on my screen door, just six feet from where I was eating. A good-sized mouse that probably occupied a comfortable home under *my* comfortable home in the woods was frantically searching every crack, hole, and possible entry point. He clearly smelled something he wanted to feast on, and I could see he meant business—he was determined to get in!

I put my meal down and just watched.

Mice are so quick, creative, and cute. One of the joys of life in the woods is observing these friendly neighbors. They're great entertainment when no TV or radio or electricity is available. I'm delighted watching this creative problem solver. He won't get in, I thought, and I will just enjoy the show!

After a considerable search over every inch of that screen door, he suddenly dropped to the floor of the porch and under the door he came—and he was next to me faster than a flash.

I don't mind mice and sometimes enjoy them. I just don't want to share my limited groceries with them. This friendship only goes so far!

This scenario called to mind the book *Life is So Good*. (If you want to know what it was really like for the race and culture of African Americans in the late 1800s and early 1900s, *Life is So Good* by George Dawson will reveal it to you in its raw, brutal, natural way.) George was the oldest of five children and grandson of a slave. Born in Marshall, Texas in 1898, he lived in a shack typical of this era. George made friends with the rats in his house and found ways to feed them from his limited food supply, sometimes even while he ate. He loved them.

I generally don't share this affinity. Jumping up, I moved toward the kitchen door, only a yard away from his position. He scampered behind the ancient kitchen door, and I closed it quickly, only to realize my shenanigans wouldn't begin to keep him out, even if the door was closed.

So, I opened the door, stomped my foot, and he quickly recalculated his position, realizing the greater part of wisdom might be for him to retreat to his safer and more comfortable environs. At least that's what I think prompted his quick exit.

Getting back to my lunch before it got any colder, I pondered where else mice had easy access to my pantry. Seeing several places of easy access, I decided to go visit another cabin's owner after lunch to see if he had any ideas for solving the problem. He loves his cabin and spends a lot of time in it when it isn't rented to others, so he keeps it amazingly tight and safe from outsiders who might like a place to spend their winter. As I suspected, he knew immediately what to do and came the next day to fix the door.

After this hour to hour-and-a-half fix, there was only one problem left. We needed a handle! Because the spring was not strong enough to hold the door closed tightly enough to keep the little critters out, the fix necessitated a screen door handle to pull it shut from the inside.

With no hardware store for 28 miles, necessity called for invention. He walked right out onto the forest floor, just a few feet from the cabin, and searched the ground for a "handle." Everything he found was too decomposed and soft to be sturdy.

Just before he arrived, I was down at the lake's edge, drinking in the sights and scenes in silence. Observing all the cedar driftwood, masterpieces of nature's art, right at my feet, I was thinking about how much I'd like to rent a U-Haul truck, pack up these masterpieces, and take them to Texas to put around my garden and fountain. We had already decorated this area with other driftwood to make it aesthetically attractive.

Then, remembering a few smaller pieces of driftwood, an idea struck. "I've been down to the water's edge observing the cedar driftwood," I told him. "It is strong, tough, sturdy and would make a great handle!"

He agreed and went to the water's edge, instantly locating a curved root that, once sawed to configuration, was a screen door handle more artistic than any you could find in a cabin supply.

The point of this wilderness tale? We need more John Wesley in our blood! Adapting this kind of frugality and creativity in solving the problems of our day-to-day lives, we can move much closer to being "God's people in the world" than we are now, and budget raising would not even be an issue. We wouldn't need it!

Of mice and doorhandles—making use of the gifts of nature

It was a crystal-clear morning, a perfect 56 degrees, with a bright moon and a scattering of stars. It was still dark when I started clearing ashes from yesterday's fire in my outside fire pit and gathering wood to build my new fire with good, fresh, hardwood that burns a long time.

I took a fresh look at the hard old birch stump I busted out yesterday. At first it was ugly as sin to look at, but now I see its beauty as I appreciate the Master Gardner's creation of the tangled root system that made such a firm foundation for this tree.

I placed this old stump on top of my newly built fire. Still wet from the inch of rain on the day before yesterday, it slowly smoked the moisture out and eventually contributed beautifully to my morning fire. As this root eventually burned to deep, red hot through and through, outer layers of red-hot embers broke away and fell deeper into the pit, contributing even more significantly to the fire.

Hot, hard embers make the fire! (Another stop sign here on the power of patience to nurture people until they are inspired to contribute.)

Taking this observation further into a metaphor for senior ministry, I have the unique and grand privilege to minister to those red-hot embers, the tangled, broad base of roots that once made the church; made our families; made our community. These are beautiful, powerful, and influential people. They are the Marys and the Marthas who have quietly behind the scenes been giants and saints and mothers and fathers; Sunday school teachers, piano teachers, secretaries, schoolteachers, etc.

One of these senior treasures that came to mind in this morning's fireside reverie was the first woman in Roosevelt's Social Security Administration in Washington. What stories she shared with me! (I wish I had slowed down long enough to record them.) They are jewels that should not be lost.

What a powerful, beautiful, hot ember who made such a difference in her lifetime—and sharing the hot embers of her experience with this young preacher whose life was deeply enriched and nurtured. What a special treat and blessing to have her here, in her 90s, the last of her family, to have the privilege and honor to tell her story to someone from her church who cared, was very interested, and for once, only listened. I wish I had learned that lesson earlier—to be quiet and listen.

I'm remembering another one of these embers, a man who once served as warden at Leavenworth prison, where the most notorious and hardened criminals are sent. He was intimate friends with Chicago and New York mafia dynasties. What priceless stories! Stories probably never recorded, maybe never even shared! Contents of a fascinating and historically significant book never written. But ol' Larry didn't have time to stop and listen (more "important" ministry to tend to; needed to get on to the next neglected senior). We all know what happens to that "I'll do it later" list.

Natural resources—the perfect stump

~ ~ ~

What would it take to adequately minister to these senior "embers" in the church or in any community?

How can we do a better job of being with them when they feel (and often are) forgotten by the care and fellowship they helped build?

How much significant ministry I have missed?

How many significant moments, experiences, opportunities for ministry get missed?

How much nurturing and support does the church miss by not being there? (Hint: More times than any of us even want to imagine.)

How many times are these stories shared only during celebrations of life, when they should be celebrated while these saints are still alive, in the places they helped to create and sustain?

CHAPTER 12

Early morning fire, long before dawn

his morning as I settled down by my roaring fire, I was immediately reminded of another of our real saints, a widow who lived alone in a simple, clean, neat, and modest home. Her daughter was very attentive to her. She had arthritis so bad she could hardly walk, use her hands, or do much of anything.

She spent most of her days sitting in her rocking chair reading her Upper Room and devouring her Bible. I could not even enter the door of her humble home without being overcome with deep admiration for this dynamic and deeply involved member of our church who refused to quit!

In talking with her, I learned that years before she worked at Convair, an American aircraft manufacturing company that later expanded into rockets and spacecraft. (In 1953 Convair became General Dynamics, then was acquired in 1997 by today's Lockheed Martin Defense and Armament Systems. I know this seems extraneous but be patient. This adds important context to the story.) One day she got a call from President Roosevelt, who asked her if she would be willing to do something special for him and our country.

Can you imagine a call and an invitation like that?

"Well, of course I can!" she replied. "Can you tell me what it is?"

"No, it is very high security," the president said. "I will have some people pick you up in a few days. You are just to follow their instructions."

Wow again! What could this mean for a patriotic American, doing her part to win a war?

As indicated, she was called a few days later, told to dress and prepare to be away from home for a while, and she was taken to the old, historic Texas Hotel at Commerce and 9th Street in downtown Fort Worth. She was sequestered there for several days, probably with an invisible eye on her, perhaps several.

Then she was instructed that she would be picked up the next morning at 3:00 a.m. to go out to the Convair plant. Once there, she was instructed to ride a bicycle carrying an auxiliary airplane gas tank and then return for a second. As instructed, she left the tanks at the plane in a secluded area.

During the process she noted the name, "Enola Gay," on the plane. It meant nothing to her, but it registered in her memory bank.

She was taken back to the hotel, held for a period longer, and then given her freedom to return to her normal activities.

Can you guess the rest of the story?

A few days after her return, she was catching up on the news from the time she was sequestered, and she read about a plane named the "Enola Gay" that dropped a bomb on Nagasaki and another one on Hiroshima.

She was numb! Shocked! She could not believe her eyes! Upon seeing this news, she immediately took a leave day from work and spent it in the chapel of our church. She prayed and prayed, repenting the sin, in her eyes, she had committed, albeit unaware. Her grief poured out as she cried out and wept. Imagine her shame. She felt guilty and mortified. She said she never told another soul.

Had she not shared it with me that day, this story of significance, this piece of US military history, of moral conundrum, would never have been heard. It is certainly a piece of history that will remain unknown.

Can you grasp how cathartic sharing a story like that was for her? What if out of her deepest remorse, this everyday saint, choir member, Sunday School teacher, faithful pledger to her church, had held it inside her until the day she died?

Forgive us, forgive us, O God! We know not what we do!

~ ~ ~

As I sat on the lake shore in total darkness, waiting for the morning light to break and begin the magical appearance of dawn on the horizon, these thoughts arose spontaneously from somewhere deep within me:

"O Lord, our Lord, how majestic . . . ."

Presence! Presence! Presence!

Then a voice followed, also from that deep interior space:

"Larry, it is a present—a gift of one more whole day!"

How shall I receive this gift and give it back to the Giver?

Only I can decide!

Just a few short hours later, in the mid-afternoon, foreboding clouds moved in fast, then gave way to a serious storm that I later learned was a hurricane. Seeking shelter in my cabin, I listened as huge trees in the nearby woods crashed to the ground, each landing with a resounding thud. I also came to recognize the distinctive crack of large, heavy branches as they were severed from their trunks and fell to the ground, often breaking into pieces as they landed.

With no way to know of this impending storm, this afternoon's hurricane caught me by surprise. Glad to be in the relative safety of the cabin, and not out in the woods, I sat still and listened as these high winds and hard rains also brought unexpected gifts.

Like manna from heaven, the firewood came. I, like Hebrews in the wilderness, received the bounty of good hardwood, garbage wood, maple, fir, and birch—all falling right into my daily path. Because of this unexpected bounty, today's fire was my best yet. What does this suggest about stepping out in faith?

~ ~ ~

"GOD, the Lord, is my strength; he makes my feet like hinds' feet, he makes me tread upon my high places." (Habakkuk 3:19 RSV)

This is a very profound verse, and I've lived with it since my called days when I read a book by Glen Clark called *Let My Feet Be As 'Hinds' Feet.* If you've ever wondered what in the world this verse means, you're not alone. You almost have to be a "wilderness guy" to have the faintest idea what the writer is saying here.

So, here's the key: a *hind* is a deer. A deer is very sure-footed, and their back feet (hind feet) always track *exactly* where the front feet go—another of God's marvels!

This "hinds' feet" reference is a metaphor that relates to our life in Christ and "being God's people in the world." How can we be sure our feet track exactly where God's tracks go?

CHAPTER 13

Infinite colors of dawn

What does this say about human nature—about my nature—that even in my lengthy stay in perfect stillness, in a perfect Garden of Eden, I found myself wanting to hurry processes that take time and patience? And very important here—what does that say about our Christian mission, ministry, and actions?

One of the gifts of silence is I will listen and seek to hear and learn from it. Does that depend on what is said?

As I watched the dawn break into an infinity of color painted in the eastern sky by the Master Artist, I sat by my 4:00 a.m. fire, thinking and trying to recapture a word and practice lost to our culture and church and spiritual lives.

Contemplation.

The industrial revolution and its accompanying "enlightenment" smothered contemplation in rational and dualistic thinking that you and I have been immersed in for decades.

Martin Luther, John Wesley, and a few others like Thomas Merton and Richard Rohr have attempted to resurrect the practice of contemplation. The Celtic Christians (John Philip Newell, etc.) have kept it alive from the second century to today.

These people, with Jesus, and many other spiritually alive, fire-in-the-belly prophets have tried to get us to see the value of contemplation—and yet, we won't see or hear; we won't listen or understand. We stay unaware.

Contemplation isn't anything new. Nor is it an old, dusty, outmoded concept. It's right here, right now, perpetually alive in this book called the Bible! Read Merton, read Rohr, and learn what contemplation is. One option for us today is to get back to contemplation and see what it does for us personally—and our church missionally.

As a church, and as a society, we have become too rational, too cultural, too dualistic to get quiet and allow Jesus to show us the Third Way: "to do justice, and to love kindness, and to walk humbly with your God." (Micah 6:8 KJV) This loss of contemplation is why the church is dying today. Wilderness, contemplation, quiet in "a great while before day" as the gospels say (Mark 1:35 KJV), is where Jesus finds space for this practice, this lost art!

What does this have to do with building my daily fire?

Here's what I noticed, observing myself as I tended my fire. When I saw my fire smoldering, I said, in my controlling, narcissistic, ego-centered way, "I'm going to get up and go make that fire work!"

So, I got up to do just that. Then God reached me in the stillness again and again and again with the (literally) blistering message, "Larry, will you kindly sit down? I know how to handle fire. I've done it a long, long time. If you need proof, look at the sun for five minutes with your bare eyes and go blind with white, white, white heat that has kept Mother Earth alive for billions of years!"

Is this a metaphor here for us about mission? Spiritual formation? Has the wilderness made me insane or brought me to sanity? Am I wrong, or am I finally seeing it Jesus' way?

I have a bias, another of my assumptions, which is always and forever necessary, appropriate, and, I think, absolutely essential. I feel that while God got through to me in the silence of the wilderness, God can do the same in Fort Worth, Texas, if I similarly change, slow down, get quiet and "Be Still . . . ." (Psalm 46:10 KJV)

He leads me beside the still waters; . . . my cup overflows." (Psalm 23:2-5 RSV) Oh God! Isn't this also possible at home in Fort Worth?

Yes, periodic retreats to the woods for tune-up would always be helpful and affirming, and then we can return and be the church God wants us to be in our day-to-day surroundings, wherever and whatever they may be.

My assumption is that God is assuring us this is possible in Psalm 8: "How magnificent is thy name in all the earth!"

> "O LORD, our Lord,
> how majestic is thy name in all the earth!
> Thou whose glory above the heavens is chanted
> by the mouth of babes and infants,
> thou hast founded a bulwark because of thy foes,
> to still the enemy and the avenger.
> When I look at thy heavens, the work of thy fingers,
> the moon and the stars which thou hast established;
> what is man that thou art mindful of him,
> and the son of man that thou dost care for him?
> Yet thou hast made him little less than God,
> and dost crown him with glory and honor.
> Thou hast given him dominion over the works of thy hands;
> thou hast put all things under his feet,
> all sheep and oxen,
> and also the beasts of the field,
> the birds of the air, and the fish of the sea,
> whatever passes along the paths of the sea.
> O LORD, our Lord,
> how majestic is thy name in all the earth!" (Psalm 8 RSV)

If this truly is our Father's world," wherever we are in it, how, oh, how do we create Pentecost, again and again and again? Consider, contemplate, muse, change, follow the ever-present Holy Spirit and "Be about my Father's business!" (Luke 2:49 KJV)

Let us humbly, prayerfully, and perhaps quietly and anonymously follow God's lead to the best of our abilities and see what evolves as God's program for ALL CREATION! Let's let God build fires in our bellies, not as in "I am helpless, God, you have to do it for me," but as Jesus put it, "Rise, take up your bed and go home." (Matthew 9:5-8 RSV) Then let us do what we can to build that fire in others to see what "great things" God will do among us. (Psalm 126:3 RSV)

When God builds a garden and tends it alone, without human hands, it is too magnificent to behold, to put into words. "On the other hand," as the Tevye character from *Fiddler on the Roof* might say, when God needs or wants a garden to feed his entire family adequately, God asks for some human cooperation from hands like ours. This garden, too, is magnificent to behold, and beyond words to adequately describe. This is the church, I think Jesus envisions for humanity!

The Celts have kept this vision alive, in part, with their contemplative worship alone and in community in the wilderness (outdoors). It seems to me that this contemplative element may be an essential ingredient that is missing in our church life today. Perhaps contemplation could resurrect us and set us free to "be God's people in the world" (as we say in our United Methodist benediction) in a new way, in a way that tends God's Garden and feeds our souls!

In my fire building, which has been so significant in stimulating my creative juices, I can build a huge, high, hot fire that is magnificent to behold with the help of nature—wood, fire, and oxygen! And I can let that fire burn on its own, never touching or tending it, and quietly, certainly, the entire woodpile will burn—and go out!

If, however, I want fire for my pleasure and inspiration, it requires me to cooperate with the universe and tend to it periodically. I keep it going. I revitalize it! I resurrect it. It takes both of us.

I see this as another very profound message in church leadership.

~ ~ ~

So many parallels between fire building and spirit building in our lives. If I crowd the logs too closely, they will burn, but not well. What does that say about my crowded schedule at church?

The logs need space around them to get oxygen to the fire. The more oxygen, the better it burns. Why do hospitals post the "Oxygen in Use" sign? Oxygen is explosive!

We all need God's oxygen to keep our fires burning. How do we get God's oxygen?

Stillness!

How much stillness do we have in our life? What I found about me is that having a quiet devotional time every day is essential. I've done this since I was a child. Every day this practice promises me a circle, quiet time that has kept my fire lit.

So even though I've had a degree of stillness for most of my life, the woods taught me that the more stillness I got, the more brightly my fire burned, and the faster the insights came to me. Is this true for everyone? I don't know, but it is for me!

There is another component here. The wilderness opened my eyes to see how much ego there was in my life and ministry that I did not see. I'd bet my bottom dollar that others saw it, but I didn't. None of us do.

And if someone said to me, "Larry, you have too much ego." I might have listened. More than likely, I would consider it and say, "I don't think so. I think you are projecting *your* ego!" (We all do that, you know.) My, how I have done it!

So how do we learn to handle ego? For me, the more I focus on authentic self and God and Spirit, the more ego dies a slow and certain death. I find that whatever gets my focus, gets me! Focus on ego and its actions and I see it everywhere. Focus on God/Spirit and who God made me to be, and the destructive force of ego fades!

~ ~ ~

It was fascinating to me how every single fire I built was somehow different. Each required a slightly different strategy. Each day I'd build my fire and say, "Oh! This is the way to do it! I'll do it this way again tomorrow!" And the next day the wood I gathered would be shaped differently, aged differently, composed differently. One piece big, one piece small. I can't build it like yesterday!

Is this like each new day God gifts to me? Today was so great, I will do this again tomorrow. But no! Circumstances aren't the same. We get fresh manna with every new day. (We're all children of Israel in the wilderness, remember?) Every day requires a new strategy. It takes a fresh walk with Jesus to get through each new day.

This can also be translated to church programming. We did it this year and it was a "home run"—so let's do it again next year! And the next year we build it the same way, but the original spark isn't there. The fire has diminished. Do it several years and it dies.

This reality also applies to our personal devotional work and spiritual practices. I think we all must constantly change and grow. We are not the same every day. We must refresh ourselves to meet new surroundings, conditions, and circumstances to learn who God is 24/7—and what God is in our lives.

I brought my supplies into the cabin in these crappy plastic bags every store continues to use. I hate them—but I compromised and used them to carry my groceries. However, I figured out a way not to allow them to get into our environment where they do so much damage. I re-used each bag for my garbage, and then every three or four days I took it out to my fire and burned the whole package, returning both the bag and its contents to mother earth for reuse in building a new person, plant, or tree!

What profound implications or metaphors can we draw from this?

Every day a new strategy

CHAPTER 14

"Be still and know that I am God." (Psalm 46:10 RSV)

Today found me considering the old gospel songs. Many of them I was raised on since I was a pup! Lots of those old gospel songs just spontaneously spring up in my mind, day after day. How atrocious the lyrics in some—and, sometimes, how wonderful the lyrics in the same song!

On this particular morning, I awakened with this partial verse, "Oh Lord, haste the day when my seeing will be sight. The clouds rolled back as the stone." I have been seeing with new eyes, myself, my world, my life, and my church—"my seeing has become sight!"

Can or does this happen without stillness—the stillness of Psalm 46:10, "Be still and know that I am God," in my life?

I for years have read Psalm 103: "Bless the Lord, O my soul; and all that is within me, bless his holy name." (Psalm 103:1 RSV) I wanted so much to live in this praise daily, throughout the day! I would try. I would work at it. I would struggle with it. I never made it work.

Paul writes in Thessalonians, "In every thing give thanks: for this is the will of God in Christ Jesus concerning you." (I Thessalonians 5:18 KJV) Same scenario for me. In some things, yes, even most. But in *every* thing? I couldn't get there. What is wrong with this old, recalcitrant reprobate?

I got my answer in the woods: Be still! *"Be still, and know that I am God."* (Psalm 46:10 KJV)

After two months of putting my attention daily on "be(ing) still" I discovered one day, "I am doing this every day, most of the day. I am 'bless(ing) the Lord, oh my soul.' It is as natural as breathing in and breathing out." No struggle, hard work, stress, or push, push, push. All I had to do was just breathe in and breathe out.

Perfect? By no means. Just better and better as the time went on.

My ordination vow was, "Are you going on to perfection?"

Of course, I said, "Yes!"

And today, I would add, "much, much too slowly."

~ ~ ~

I have friends here in the woods who live in a common-law relationship. They appear to enjoy each other—and life—very fully. One day he said, "We don't know much about your God." Then he said, "Pause. Look up at the treetops and sky." Then he added, "It just doesn't get much better than this!" He says this with such passion, honesty, and joy in his voice and face. She is less verbal, but I get the same message from her non-verbally.

More than once I wanted to ask them, "How do you do this? What motivates you to be this way?" But I didn't ever feel intuitively right about doing this. Mainers are a different breed from Texans. Many of them will do about anything for you to help you out. They are hospitable, caring, open, and honest. *And* they also appear to live by a "I don't want to know you too well" credo.

If I were to ask these questions, my sense is they would honestly and openly say, "Oh, I don't know. I am just this way."

And I think that is true. This is their nature. This is their standard value system. How does church, Christ, and religion fit into this?

I would like to know.

~ ~ ~

"Go to the ant, thou sluggard; consider her ways, and be wise." (Proverbs 6:6 KJV)

Sitting at 10:30 a.m. beside my pit fire, I see a small black ant—at least half the size of a black carpenter ant—about the size of a small red ant. He was struggling up a large granite stone with a load of something black at least twice his size.

He'd struggle up the steep rock, then roll to the bottom. He'd get up immediately and do the same thing, time after time. I am dropping all other plans for today to follow this little energetic, strong, creature of God, I decided.

When he finally got near the top, headed in the direction his GPS must have said to go, he encountered heat he did not like. He turned to the side, went across the rock sideways, rolled to the ground, and started off in a more northerly direction.

He was really struggling with that heavy load. He would encounter the carpet of pine needles on the ground or lichens on a granite rock, and his load would get hung up on some obstacles. He'd pull and tug until the load gave way and soon had to repeat this process, over and over again.

It was hard work, slow progress, and he was determined, without rest, to get his load to its destination (who knows where). After about eight feet of going north, he turned east, down my steep embankment from the cabin to the lake. Soon he was headed into a small forest of young Douglas firs and Scotch pine seedlings, two-to-four-feet high.

I got off my chair, laid down on the ground nearby and followed his slow, laborious progress. Sometimes, when his load really got stuck in the thick carpet of pine needles, he'd pull and pull, always backwards, I guess because of the size and weight of his load. Each time, he would pull until he broke loose from his load, and then he'd go on a search mission, as if pondering: "Now, which way can I go to free my load and get on the way?" He'd always find a way, and with intense effort, go back and get his load and get moving again.

When I got up close to inspect what his cargo was, I saw it was probably the dead queen of his colony. She was at least twice as large. He was so determined, all alone, to complete some sort of mission with his dead queen.

After another hour of long, slow, labor-intensive travel, he finally made it to what I supposed was his den. There were many other ants there his size. It was a nice, high mound with a good-sized hole at its top.

Then, strangely, he turned around, still carrying his load, and started back up the steep hill—an even more labor-intensive path. I watched him go for about six feet. It appeared he was going to retrace his steps down the incline. Why?

Since I had already watched him for more than an hour and a half, had no way of understanding anything more of what was going on—and it was well past lunch time and I was very hungry—I decided, "Enough is enough! Go eat!"

CHAPTER 15

Birds, chipmunks, and a kangaroo mouse

This morning I noticed quite a spread of light ashes and dirt, about a foot square, just outside the rocks of the pit. I had just gotten up and made my way to the fire pit to build my daily fire. It was windy, so I reasoned that these ashes must have blown over the rocks during the night. Then I forgot about it.

There was one other thing that drew my attention, though. There was a perfect little hole about the size of a quarter at the outer edge of the ashes outside the pit. "Maybe some small animal of the forest has a home down there," was my passing thought.

However, I had been sitting in this same spot for days and had not noticed a hole there before. This seemed to be a small issue. Sometimes I'm not that aware.

I built my fire and soon had a nice blaze going. It was pitch dark, an overcast night. As I leaned back in my chair to enjoy my morning cup of coffee before a beautiful fire, out of the left corner of my eye I saw something move. I turned in that direction, reaching for my flashlight, and then the brightness of the fire revealed a small kangaroo mouse darting into that little hole.

And just about as fast as he entered the hole, he reappeared. He stuck his little head up with those black, glossy, beady eyes, inspecting me and the fire as if to inquire, "Just what is this that has appeared near my home? Am I safe? What goes here?"

Then he came out of the hole, stopped near it, and just eyeballed me, face to face. My left foot was about two inches from him and his hole.

After this short reconnaissance moment, I guess he decided he was safe enough to continue his activity. And frenetic activity it was! He would leap with those long back legs to a nearby spot of pine needles and decaying leaves under a patch of young Douglas fir and Scotch pine trees just starting their life in the forest. Then just as fast, he'd dart back to his hole with one or the other of these items, headed down his hole.

The longer I just sat there, motionless, watching this process, the more intriguing it got. Very frequently his body and that leaf or needle was too large for the hole.

"What kind of problem is this?" he seemed to say. "None at all! I've been here before!"

More dirt started flying at the edge of the hole as these four legs spun like a 4x4 pick-up stuck in the sand, and in a moment the process was ended, deposited in his little luxury condominium, and out of his hole he went for more.

This went on for at least 30 minutes. By now my old size ten-and-a-half walking shoe was no issue. He started darting across it as if climbing a rock, a short cut to his nesting material.

Then it became even more intriguing. He commenced to dig a bit larger hole at the entrance. Then he came out about six inches and dug up loose dirt in a circle around his entrance, now kicking the dirt *toward* the entrance hole. That task completed, he started on his loose dirt pile, pushing it into the hole.

"Oh!" I thought. "He has prepared his winter house. He's going to cover it up because it is well marked for him between two small stones. Then later in the fall he'll open his condo and snuggle in for the winter."

Now, by this time I had put together another piece of the puzzle. I had brought with me a bird feeder with wild bird mix in it that I had hung between two trees on a wire. After two weeks of not one bird visiting it, even though they are everywhere in the area—in abundance, I took it down, put it on the ground, and said, "I will just feed it to the chipmunks. They love this stuff, especially the sunflower seeds."

I had put it about three feet behind me, near the porch, so I could watch the activity. However, after about three days I saw no activity. I could tell from the diminishing bird seed, however, that there had been considerable interest in its quick trip convenience.

It dawned on me that this mouse, only about two and a half inches long and as cute as a bug, had probably hoarded an entire winter of groceries, carried it all down into his cozy home, and was very well-stocked for the season.

Going back to the hole clearing, I realized my assumption about what was transpiring was wrong! After covering his entrance smoothly, where it appeared that no hole ever existed, he poked his little nose through the entrance, entered, disappeared completely, and then reappeared almost instantly. This happened three or four times. Cover the hole until ground was flat, enter, exit, and do it again.

"What in the world is he doing?" I wondered as he entered the nearly clogged hole yet again. I waited, realizing I was holding my breath—and he didn't come back out!

At this point I had completely forgotten about my fire and the breaking of dawn that I thoroughly enjoyed each day. I got to see this miracle of nature unfold in real time!

As I stood there marveling, a large bulge appeared at the entrance of the hole. Was the mouse coming out again?

No! As I watched, transfixed, the bulge gradually diminished until there was no sign of dirt movement, and the top of the hole was level with the rest of the ground around it. He had put in for the winter. Inside that hole, packed as tightly as his little mouse frame could make it, he was fixed in luxury for a long, safe hibernation!

Now how often would a gift of nature like this be observed by a human? This little master architect had systematically and quickly prepared for the winter with a very well-designed and precisely executed step-by-step procedure. What engineering. What planning and preparation—and what exquisite, comfortable, safe, and warm accommodations he had!

I wondered whether he knew (was this why he chose this location?) that this cabin and its adjacent fire pit is used year-around by both summer vacationers and winter sports enthusiasts. So, even when the temp is 20 or 30 below on top of the ground, the mouse's little home gets warmed every time a fire is built!

Throughout this one-to-two-hour process I assumed a variety of things about what was going on. Nearly every one of them proved wrong. Is there a lesson here about the assumptions and belief systems each of us carries around in our head? And do we check them for accuracy?

CHAPTER 16

Human ingenuity and logs ready for tow

You might think that here in the natural surroundings of the North Maine Woods, all my awe would be directed at God's creation—the natural world. But as I sit here today, hearing, then at last seeing a giant diesel truck carrying 100,000 pounds of logs as if they were marshmallows, I can't help but shift some of that awe toward the unnatural world of human ingenuity. We were created in God's image—so we're made to create. To engineer, even. But when I think of what kind of engineering it must have taken to create some of the heavy logging equipment that routinely rumbles past my camp, it is almost impossible for me to fathom.

Huge forestry harvest crews were working within my hearing when wind was from the north. They have a machine with a quarter-inch-thick saw blade that weighs nearly a ton and can cut down a 100-to-150-year-old tree ninety feet tall in seconds, strip the limbs, and then cut the trunk into ten-, twenty-, or fifty-foot lengths in just minutes. I wanted very much to see that machine in action, but I had no wheels.

How many men, 100 years ago, working all winter long, in Maine, did it take to fell a giant tree, especially a maple, birch, oak—hard, hard hardwood? This is especially relatable to me today, as I just spent hours trying to trim the jagged twigs and bark off a maple branch I found to use as a walking stick. Using my sharp, sharp knife I could only barely nick the wood, chipping away bit by bit.

Today, one man with one piece of machinery goes into the woods and cuts huge trees with a giant, sharp circular blade maybe 20 to 25 feet in diameter. Then this machine will shift that same blade to a different angle and trim away the huge limbs down next to the trunk (a giant version of my walking stick). Then, still with the same machine, two huge, sharp wheels trim all the remaining burs and branches, creating a 40-to-60-foot log looking as smooth as a wooden light pole.

Then giant cranes pick up these enormous logs like toothpicks, put them on a *porcupine*, a semi-trailer specially designed to carry these enormous loads of heavy timber, and repeat this process until it's a full load. Then the next giant diesel truck pulls up to be filled. What magnificent engineering ingenuity it took to create these giant pieces of machinery that work together so efficiently!

Then I think, if human ingenuity is capable of doing this amazing work in a forest, what could it make possible in the church?

~ ~ ~

After living on Porter Point for three weeks, this morning I discovered a pile of cut and split hardwood logs, perfect for keeping my fire going, plus a stack of softwood logs, probably a three-day supply! I must have walked past this woodpile (in search of firewood) at least a half-dozen times each day for three weeks. And it is about one-third of my walk to the other wood supply I've been frequenting—much shorter!

Why am I just seeing it for the first time this morning?

My piercing questions are:

- How much of the Divine am I walking past daily in search of enlightenment?

- What else is right beside, within, or all around me that I'm walking by and not seeing or aware of?

- Drilling down to the "why," is it because I won't slow down long enough to notice what is around me?

Contemplating this, I remember the black carpenter ant I watched for three days, and I discover a new parallel. Frantically searching for a way off the porch and back to the ground, every six inches he stepped over a crack that could easily have returned him to earth and not touch any part of his body. Am I any different?

There were also knotholes in the floor and baseboards, large enough for a medium-large mouse to enter or exit—and he never saw these opportunities to get what he needed, either. All day (and I assume all night), he kept searching for a way home, missing a variety of perfect solutions all around him.

What a pregnant metaphor to consider as I rush through my busy, "I'll never get it all done" days.

~ ~ ~

A more comfortable venue

On this cold, drizzly morning in the second week of September I got up at about 3:00 a.m. to solid darkness and an overcast 51 chilly degrees. I said to myself, as I always do, "I'm going to have my pit fire!"

So, I got busy and built my fire, and then, because it was raining, chose to sit inside my screened-in porch that sits about 10 to 12 feet from my fire pit. It's almost as sitting next to the fire, right?

Wrong! I was freezing my tail off!

So, by 4:30 that afternoon I folded up camp and moved everything inside. Using my ash shovel to bring in a hot coal, I fired the cabin's 1890s wood stove to set myself up to enjoy a much more comfortable change of venue.

In fact, I enjoyed it so much that I took a mattress off the bunk bed and made myself a bed by the wood fire and spent the whole night beside my good warm companion—an ancient, primitive, and very efficient wood stove!

To stay comfortable on the ground, I put four layers of clothing on my top half, two layers on my bottom half clear down to my toes, and I stayed toasty comfy all night long.

Around 5:00 a.m. the next morning, I got up and saw I had a clear sky and a gorgeous prospect for a sunrise. I went out to my fire pit and played out the same ritual of the day before, except no rain meant I could stay close to my pit fire—always my first choice!

About six o'clock a.m. I went on my quarter-mile hike to my woodpile and main camp, to return with four more pieces of good firewood—my capacity for this extended walk.

I dressed in layers to start the morning, then began stripping down, layer by layer as the temperature rose. Before leaving to get firewood, I took off my third layer of top, still wearing two layers below. I quickly changed my mind and put the third layer back on, took off down the path, got my wood, and returned.

Two hours later I repeated the process, but by this time I had eliminated all but one layer of clothing. Now, because the outer layer I was wearing was identical to what I wore two hours before, you would look at me and say, "Nothing has changed about him." Right?

Well, something *had* changed. I was dressed differently underneath, but only I knew that!

So, here's the point of this whole saga: In Mark 1, Jesus said to the healed leper, "See that you say nothing to any one." (Mark 1:44 RSV) Be quiet! Be anonymous! Had he done that, only careful observations would have revealed that this was a very different man.

Is this not also true of you and me as we let God's transforming love change us? We look the same on the outside, but we are different *underneath* our outer appearance.

When Jesus says, "say nothing to any one" he is telling us to listen, learn, and transform quietly. Another powerful metaphor from the woods.

Sitting in the light of my oil lamp in an antique rocking chair made from tree branches—old, old, old, and sturdy as iron, I watched the last ray of another magnificent day fade into darkness.

~ ~ ~

I awakened to build my fire just before the first rays of light crept into the eastern sky. It was an overcast morning with clouds. At last, light began to pierce small holes here and there in the overcast sky. Then, before too long, these holes began to enlarge and brighten with the beautiful light of one more, brand-new day. Then I watched in complete awe as the still-water mirror of the lake reflected those halos of light.

With the profusion of shoreline trees partially blocking my view of the water's reflections, these bright and sparkly anomalies appeared to me as the light of God coming into the world. Perhaps another metaphor from the woods.

Each denomination of the Christian church offers its own reflections, colorations of God's light. All monotheistic religions reflect God's light coming into the world in ways that are meaningful to the culture surrounding them—and all reflect but a fraction of it.

And, to carry this metaphor even further, this unique reflection of God's light is also offered by *every* person. We all reflect a part of this eternal light, and each of us reflects but a fraction of it!

≈ ≈ ≈

When I get too close to the flames in my somewhat flimsy fireside chair (painful confession—rue the day!) I get smoke in my eyes. It is not comfortable. I have to back off.

How might this metaphor relate to church?

My selfishness! My controlling! My challenges! My opportunities! My infinite possibilities! My life of spiritual formation!

There is a rich, full story in each of the above observations. God is so much bigger than what my mind can conceive.

≈ ≈ ≈

As today's dawn moved into sunrise, I noticed the overcast lifting from the east, allowing a band of bright red light to peek through the thin ribbon of clear sky exposed miles and miles away. It was magnificent to behold, thrilling to watch and contemplate. It stretched from straight east where I had clear vision, left to right as far as the forest would allow me to observe it.

Oh! But wait! Be patient, Larry! Give God a bit more time to finish the canvas of the eastern sky for the gift of one more day.

Gradually, NOW moment by NOW moment, the sky turns to a brilliant red. Then within a few more NOW moments, to a glittering gold, eventually growing too bright to observe with the human eye as old Ol' Sol (the sun) once again peeked over the tops of the forest trees on the other side of the lake.

The morning serenade of the loons sang their "good morning, new day, and thank you, Creator!" song from the sweet acoustics of their nearby cove, their own "Hallelujah Chorus".

To me this is a metaphor that speaks of a new day, new age, new millennium, and new paradigm in our world where we will be kinder to our environment and to one other.

"Let there be peace on Earth."

≈ ≈ ≈

Each day I burn old, soft "garbage wood" with the fresher hardwoods to help the Porter Camp owners to burn down threatening timber to protect their property.

Also, I love big fire.

I like to watch, listen, and grow my awareness with each new fire and its fresh message that is always there when I am willing to be still and allow our Creator to, in the words of the 1895 Clara Scott hymn, "Open my eyes that I may see; open my ears that I may hear; open my heart that I may love!"

Looking between red-hot logs, it occurs to me that when you give that old, soft, deteriorating log enough time it will turn beet-red through and through. It smolders, hotter and hotter, as I feed the fire. It won't usually flame, but it contributes profoundly to the beauty and freshness of the fire.

"Larry, are you willing to be an old, soft, decaying log that smolders, hotter and hotter, to contribute to the freshness of the church's fire as you near your eighth decade? I can and I will use you, should you take the freedom I have given you and choose to let me set you aglow. That kind of love can still do much!"

≈ ≈ ≈

"Be still, and know that I am God." (Psalm 46:10 RSV)

Sitting in the perfect silence, stillness, and peace of the woods, listening to the soft, warm purr of the fire, I allow the enrichment of those miracle flames to open my spiritual senses as I practice and learn stillness.

I have unknowingly built a huge reservoir of stress in my body I was not aware of until I got still, before my daily fires, for an *extended* period of time.

Then comes another message in the stillness: "Take no thought for the morrow . . ."

"Will you learn, Larry, to sit still and let me manage the fire (which I know how to do; consider your daily source of life—the sun)?"

"When I tell you, tend the fire!"

"Need I remind you of how often you have attempted to control life, people, and situations? How well did you do with that?"

Hmmmm.

~ ~ ~

Watching a fire that has burned for four hours and is nearing a totality of hot coals, I notice an orange flame periodically curling up from the bottom side of the biggest log like a natural curl of hair.

In time, this orange curling flame creates a very hot burning coal that will eventually drop from the log to create more heat to keep the fire burning. This intriguing process also allows the hot coal to renew its natural task, to begin heating a new coal. This process is repeated until the log has totally disappeared, returned to pure energy. As I sit back to consider this process, listening to the songs of the loons, a question occurs:

Larry? How do *you* fit this metaphor?

Processing what I've learned through all this fireside musing:

God can handle fire by God's self, with the sun, lightning, forest fires, etc.

I can handle fire alone, for the most part.

And God and I together? The result is exquisite!

Have you from time to time sensed a Divine truth and knew it was there, but you could never quite find the right words to verbalize it?

This has always been so true for me. Three months in the woods gave me the thrilling, exciting words—felt deep in my gut, "This is it!"

This fireside insight is a good illustration of one of these big ideas of faith that I have always felt or sensed but could never quite articulate.

~ ~ ~

One profound gift of silence is my sense of a much deeper, more personal relation to Jesus.

I've not had a sense of this for a long time, and this time in the woods has been, for me, one of those "this is it!" experiences.

This level of personal relationship to Jesus is so real—and so much like conversing with Patty, or via what we counselors call *chair dialogue*.

So much profound humor (i.e., fires and my need for control)!

"Let me handle it, Larry!"

"Larry, you're surprised I did it so well?"

I learned again and again in the woods of God's exquisite sense of humor. Sometimes quiet and subtle; other times loud and overpowering—and always nurturing!

A great example of this is our daily conversations at the fire pit, when we joust about who should do what with the fire and when.

"Larry, if I can handle fire, which I have done for billions of years, in cosmos, sun, forest, sky, and lightning, will you trust me enough to show you how to live an ever-transforming life that is real, natural, spontaneous, free, relaxed, and in the moment? For eternity!"

I then have a decision to make!

~ ~ ~

"Larry, I want you to really hear this and let it settle into your bones:

Talk a lot less.

Listen a lot more.

When my people hear my voice and say, 'Yes,' they will begin to live an authentic, spontaneous, in-the-moment, Naked Now.

I won't let you see me at work.

I can only be seen in retrospect as you get quiet, reflect, and say, 'Oh! You were there and I knew it not!'"

CHAPTER 17

Hauling wood—and the limits of endurance

I have debated many times in my own head the idea of euthanasia.

In my own experiences I have seen great love grow out of deep, profound suffering. Love that never would have been experienced personally, deeply, eternally without that exercise of suffering.

And what suffering, anguish, despair, depression, helplessness, hopelessness, "I am with nothing," are honestly and deeply and personally experienced by both people (of a couple) or more (in a family).

I have seen families deciding with open, caring, loving dialog that euthanasia is the way to go. They lovingly, carefully, prayerfully plan all the different rituals they, as a family, wish to include in the event. There are many and different and personally created rituals to surround this event.

Then ultimately, they lovingly, prayerfully, and joyfully experience together the final ritual, and it is as magnificent a worship experience as one will ever encounter. I have also seen and personally experienced this ritual in capital punishment, and it is and can be a profound worship experience there, as well.

Is the above issue tragic? Yes! Is it necessary? No! Is life imprisonment appropriate? Yes! Is rehabilitation and release appropriate? Yes! We have the tools and skills to do it—why, oh why will we not use them?

Back to euthanasia. Is there a right or wrong way to die?

God says, "You decide. I'll love you the same either way you go. Nothing in all creation can separate me from you!"

~ ~ ~

Two weeks from just about now I will be on a plane to return to Fort Worth. There is a part of me that is truly ready to return and enjoy Patty, my kids, my staff, my groups, my counselees, my seniors—my intimate, intimate accountability cell!

Some of me, however, is not ready for this. The part that wants to experience the excitement, joy, and further transformation of the kindergarten start I have taken here in the woods.

Will I keep my peaceful, relaxed, listen-and-act process?

Will I be able to foster *there* the whole new sense of freedom I have experienced in leaps and bounds *here*?

Will I keep my focus on the Center that will help me do all the above and much more?

Will I quietly, anonymously, and prayerfully carry the presence of God any place I go—and be aware of God's presence in every encounter I have with each person?

Will I hold deeply anchored in my nervous system the gentle, clear, sharp, loud croon of my loons as I live out each day?

These and many more issues are to be faced, decided upon, and practiced to keep this fire I've built with God burning, glowing, and growing within me.

After two and a half months in the woods, practicing listening to the silence of the forest; practicing relaxation purposefully to reduce my hidden or undetected stress; practicing the freedom I think Christ came to give us all, I was still shocked to discover how naturally and normally I put stress back into my body! How deep is this very destructive habit and learning?

I can joyfully walk along my quarter-mile, canopied path, carrying a very appropriate amount of wood. I can relax and say to myself, "Peace, Larry, peace," and feel the tension just melt from my body. Of course, it takes a certain amount of tension and stress to walk and to carry an armload of wood. And yet, when I say, "Peace," I free a bundle of unneeded stress for the walk and the task!

I'm reversing a lifetime of old messages, carried forever in my head:

"Larry, if you are going to do it, do it right!"

"The only way to succeed in life is to work hard!"

"You are a PK (preacher's kid). I don't want you to (fill in the blank)! It reflects poorly on the family, the church, and you as a person."

"You know, Larry, you have to really be strong in life."

"Keep your feelings to yourself."

"Don't say too much and let them know how dumb you really are."

It's so important to be authentic, real, and to behave in ways that are natural to you—and not according to some distorted idea of family and how a family or the individuals in it should behave or be.

We say and we sing, "Oh Lord, Most High!" (In the hymn, "Day Is Dying in The West") I have sung that thoughtfully—and thoughtlessly—many times.

In my fresh awareness in the woods, I question, "What does this mean?"

In one sense, "Lord Most High" is accurate—as a high model for *living*, not "up high in the heavens," as I have long visioned this phrase.

The woods have continued to affirm to me that *this* Lord is very low! This Lord is in the mundane, in the secular, and each moment of my life, whether I am aware of it or not.

So, I sing this song to myself often in the woods, because all the words in it resonate with what I am experiencing, right here, right now. How grateful I am that we have this hymn and that I remember most of its text.

And I sing it now with a profound new meaning!

≈ ≈ ≈

As I walked back up my three-quarter-mile path carrying an eight-foot and a six-foot log in my hands, it didn't take too long to realize I was pushing the limits of my endurance.

About one-third of the way, I stopped at a convenient granite boulder just right for a bench, right next to the path, to rest and reconsider: "Can I take both logs—or just one?"

Looking up from my deliberation, I followed the sound of a motorboat zipping across the lake toward the landing pier. I have lived for a month, right next to the pier, and I have seen almost everything that goes on there. I've watched countless episodes of loading and unloading to go to a cabin on an island, returning with equipment, returning home, or sometimes just docking to go 30 miles to get gas and groceries and water. So, as I sat on my rock bench to rest as I often did, I began my usual little guessing game: "I bet I know what they are doing."

One lesson I experienced here, is about just watching. I am probably a quarter of a mile from them, watching them through a forest clearing, and they don't have any idea that someone is studying them.

Not to record or judge, like my Ma would, quizzing me as I went to bed, before our prayer (What did you do today that I should be aware of?), and not in a creepy voyeuristic way (as a "Peeping Larry"), but could this watching from afar be like the One who watches, sees, hears, and notices every move every one of *us* makes?

This watchful eye, I have learned and now believe, likewise watches me every second without my slightest awareness.

This observer watches me with prevenient grace, instant forgiveness, unconditional love, and the absolute trust that I will do my best to handle whatever I am facing in a loving, accepting way—of myself or another. What a comfort, joy, and confidence this adds to my life when I remember it, when I feel this loving presence watching me through my days.

My desire is that every one of God's family of humankind, all 6.8 billion of them, might know this feeling, believe its deep truth, and practice this awareness, regardless of their specific concept of God.

≈ ≈ ≈

When I build a fire, I like to see action. I like flames. I like to see *progress*.

However, I have discovered that the power and effectiveness of fire is really in the quiet, those red-and white-hot coals at the bottom of the pit. Not spectacular at all! But that's what gets the job done.

Is this my role as a staff person at the church? Stay quietly in the background, practice the Christian disciplines, encourage the laity to move out there with the spectacular fires—and I am the silent resource to help get the job done? Am I to be one of the many red-and-white-hot coals that enable ministry to get done?

I was burning garbage wood. It is soft. Bugs, ants, termites, and other special small creatures and microorganisms have been doing their divine task of turning that log into rich, fertile soil that will help grow other trees, plants, flowers, fruit, etc.

As I watched my fire's progress, it looked like nothing was happening. There were few, if any, flames. I saw a very few hot coals on the outer layers of the wood. And with every nice puff of breeze, I would see a rich, hot glow down to the center, sometimes through the entire log. Hot, red coals, burning away, doing what they are supposed to do to transform the wood to something new.

This is my role in the church. You don't see my work/influence. Occasionally, however, a puff of insight breaks through and reveals my hardworking, transformative glow!

It is fascinating to watch the curling orange and blue flames as they gracefully, naturally, relaxedly, and peacefully go about *their* significant task in the fire.

Contemplate that, Larry! It has volumes to say to you!

~ ~ ~

"The Lord is my rock, my fortress, and my deliverer, my God, my rock in whom I take refuge, my shield, and the horn of my salvation, my stronghold." (Psalm 18:2 RSV)

At about the halfway point of my quarter-mile canopied road toward main camp was a nice, big, relatively smooth granite rock that was just park bench height. When I was fatigued or had an armload of wood a bit too heavy (I push the limits), I would stop at my "God rock" to enjoy its lovely view of the lake through the forest trees. This vantage point offered a clear view of the pier where people were getting into and out of their boats to get to their island cabins.

When it was raining, particularly in the late afternoon, there were times the sun, shining through the trees and upon the water from behind the rain drops, created the spectacular effect of diamonds falling from the sky. Just another wilderness reminder of blessings that sparkle during and after the rain or storm, visible to us only when we stop, get quiet, watch, listen, process, and understand!

~ ~ ~

On one occasion, as I was picking up an armload of the very heavy hardwood (the heaviest), out of habit I pushed my limits and added, "just one more piece."

I knew instinctively, "this is a wrong move, Larry! It puts too much stress on a back that needs *nurturing*, not pushing."

When I stood to return to my cabin, that "one more piece" rolled right off my arm, and I was so grateful that it did. If it had not, I would have pushed my body beyond a healthy limit.

This prompted my eternal question, debated many times in my head, to arise yet again: "Was that a pure accident? Or was it something else?"

I have experienced events that prompted this question in countless ways throughout my life. I have posed this questioned again and again internally, I have posed it with others, and I have repeated it again and again when reading certain passages of the Bible and other stimulating reading.

As I reflect on it now, in this circumstance, it seems beyond the credible to say, "those are all accidents." There has been too much order to these events to call them "coincidence." There have been too many unbelievable opportunities (even this time in the wilderness magically falling into place after so many years of thwarted effort).

I could not have planned, nor *would* I have planned for these events to unfold as they did. Yet, when I look back and ask, "How did this happen?" I extrapolate the answer: it is yet another mystery.

"Larry, and at the center of life, *all* is mystery!" came the voice from within I have come to recognize a lot more readily.

So, ultimately, it appears to me that *mystery is* the only answer to my lifelong question that has been debated since Job, and I am sure, long before that. It is at the heart of so much debate, division, war, and destruction today.

Can this basic question ever be answered definitively? My sense is that it can't. Should it be answered? I don't think so. I think it's more important to learn to live with the mystery.

It is in our honest, open debate—discussion and evolving experiences of life—that our differences of opinion on basic issues, with the right tools, can lead to reconsideration, wholeness, healing, intimacy, and deep, meaningful friendships—plus a vital faith to live by!

~ ~ ~

One of the most amazing wonders of the wilderness to me is how nature and God (Is there really any difference or are they one and the same?) keep the forest plant and animal life in such perfect balance.

I can see this balance anywhere and everywhere I look in these woods.

One example is the tree population. I am here in July, August, and September, the best growing season in Maine. Gardens usually don't bear fruit here until the end of July.

From where I was situated in the woods, I saw a multitude of new trees bursting from the ground in settings ideal for this to happen. I am sure they are in the thousands, if not millions—pine, birch, maple, oak, and more.

The summer's heat and drought will eliminate some. Winter's harshness will take its toll. As they begin to mature and need more light and sunshine to grow, the shade of older trees will eliminate many more. And at times, disease does the same. Then come threats such as lightning, forest fires, and beavers building dams. Beaver dams creating bogs—and then acres and acres of trees die from too *much* water. The life-or-death drama seems endless.

And the forest, if left alone, will continuously heal, renew, and become a virgin forest again! What kind of mind? What kind of planning? What kind of management accomplishes all of this?

We are into the mystery once again—and how pervasive, in all the cosmos, is God's healing and nurturing love!

≈ ≈ ≈

Studying Mark's gospel in this wilderness, I became more acutely aware of what Mark repeatedly calls to our attention: Jesus always taught using stories that fit the experience and maturity of his listeners.

"With many such parables he spoke the word to them, as they were able to hear it; he did not speak to them without a parable, but privately to his own disciples he explained everything." (Mark 4:33-34 RSV)

Or, as Steve Jobs said, "The most powerful person in the world is the storyteller. The storyteller sets the vision, values, and agenda of an entire generation that is to come."

≈ ≈ ≈

The story of Jesus quieting the sea is useful for explaining the concept of slowing down, relaxing, feeling peace, and carrying stillness inside. Part of learning to do these things is developing habits and practices. Mentally imaging this scene can also help:

On that day, when evening had come, he said to them, "Let us go across to the other side." And leaving the crowd, they took him with them in the boat, just as he was. And other boats were with him. And a great storm of wind arose, and the waves beat into the boat, so that the boat was already filling. But he was in the stern, asleep on the cushion; and they woke him and said to him, "Teacher, do you not care if we perish?" And he awoke and rebuked the wind, and said to the sea, "Peace! Be still!" And the wind ceased, and there was a great calm. He said to them, "Why are you afraid? Have you no faith?" And they were filled with awe, and said to one another, "Who then is this, that even wind and sea obey him?" (Mark 4:35-41 RSV)

~ ~ ~

The Gift of a New Day! The Gift of a New Day! The Gift of a New Day!

These words meant one thing before I came to Maine. They have an entirely different connotation for me now. I do not know how to put this fully into words.

I do believe embracing this daily gift to be an experience of epiphany for me. Learning to recognize each new day as a gift doesn't have to be in Maine. It doesn't even have to be a wilderness epiphany. Or does it?

Big question here! Maybe it does! Or maybe it's just easier to see and recognize in the natural world, God's first sanctuary.

So, here's a big part of my dilemma about sharing my story. When someone has not experienced something personally (such as long loon calls at 4:00 a.m. in a pitch-dark Porter Cove), how can they truly understand what I'm telling them about it?

What I seek to say is, I know people can read what I have to say about my wilderness wonderings and epiphanies in nature with varying degrees of interest, but I really don't know how to help them understand it on a deeper level.

Perhaps the object of this sharing, then, is to entice others to set their own stage for their own experience of stillness and wonder in God's natural World—God's first Bible—for themselves, in whatever place or manner means the most to *them*. For me, I knew from my first visit to Maine that this was the right setting for my exploration.

Not everyone can (or wants to) go to the North Maine Woods for three months to immerse in complete stillness and contemplation. But I believe the need is embedded within each of us to search out and find our own little piece of the wilderness to launch this exploration in our own lives.

If you want to find your wilderness, you will find it. If you don't, you won't. Maybe the wilderness is just a change of scenery—any "pause button" you can find in the busyness of your life. Giving yourself the freedom to do that and be with yourself instead of other noises and other people around you to muddy the water.

No, you don't have to go to Maine to find this kind of intimate connection with God and nature, but it sure is nice if you can!

~ ~ ~

"Hear this, Larry! You can build a beautiful fire. You can thoroughly enjoy it, for a while. However, you must add new life, fresh fuel, to it daily in order for it to continue to burn brightly and in the way you so deeply enjoy. When new life, fresh fuel, is not added to it regularly, it diminishes, then diminishes more, and ultimately dies away! Please always remember this!"

Immediately I recognized the metaphor—and the connection with the fresh manna received daily by God's people wandering in the wilderness.

We all need fresh manna—new life for our spirit—every day. New life for the church, new life for small groups, every day. Everyone needs fresh manna daily; yesterday's manna is sour, worthless!

CHAPTER 18

Listen. Can you hear the loons?

O ver and over and over, a distinctive refrain rings all around me in the early dawn of each new day in the woods. There is a cadence in the loon's yodel that, to me, fits these words perfectly: "I thank you, God!"

"All nature sings and around me rings the beauty of thy sphere!"

Following perfect silence for about 15 minutes I hear the faint, distinctive, recognizable call, "I thank you, God" in the distance, from away down the cove, as Mr. Loon pronounces his praise to another part of the world. I wait a few more minutes, and this beautiful call is closer, and then, it's right beside me as Mr. Loon goes for his early morning meander across the waters. He moves up and down the cove in this way each morning, praising his creator and announcing the gift of a new day.

~ ~ ~

Reflecting on what three months in the wilderness has done for me, there's one biggie that comes immediately to mind. I feel I have moved much closer to peace and patience—and away from my earlier compulsion and control.

Dr. Wayne Oats, one of my early mentors, once told me, "You have to be a compulsive person to be a good minister." My, did *that* stab me in the heart—and set my course for a high-stress life of ministry. I saw the fallacy of this ideology clearly even then—and this was in the late '60s—but I did not question it. Instead, I adopted this mindset as standard operating procedure (SOP). (See the truth, but don't allow it to set you free!)

So, I have lived with compulsion for more than 50 years. The woods helped me drop a few "scales from my eyes" (Acts 9:18 RSV) to see a bit more clearly. I still "see through a glass, darkly;" (I Corinthians 13:12 KJV), but not quite as darkly as before!

~ ~ ~

"Larry, do you want to retain the fire, peace, patience, and joy you found in this wilderness?"

I've read that if you stay with the same statements or ideas for 21 days, they'll become part of you for the rest of your life. These mantras are for us to create, from within ourselves. I decided to take the multitude of little mantras I have listed for three months, recite them again and again, moment by moment for the next 21 days until they are mine forever!

For me—and from my experiences working with others through decades of pastoral counseling—it's important to be authentic and real in writing these mantras and to create what feels natural in our individual situations. Everyone is different and every situation is different, and the ideas we need to attach ourselves to—the changes we want to make in our life—are the things we want to write down. These understandings can be fleeting, coming spontaneously in our times of silence and contemplation, and in writing them down and keeping them close for the 21 days, these mantras can become a part of who we are through our deliberate intent.

This, I think, is where mantra, affirmation, and intentions crisscross. When you make something a *mantra*, the emphasis is on sameness, repetition, *ingraining* that thought or idea. An *affirmation* is a positive thought or truth or assertion you want to incorporate into your awareness to change patterns of thinking or awareness. *Intent*, I'd say, is wrapped up in all of it—the overarching desire or impetus for change.

When Jesus went to the wilderness, was this what he was doing?

~ ~ ~

I also learned something about the devil in the woods:

He ain't "out there" . . . he is "in here!"

Forget about fighting the demons "out there," Larry, face those demons where they really are—"in here!"

~ ~ ~

The deeper I move into stillness, the more vivid and alive I feel in my faith walk.

The incredible promise?

There is always more silence, stillness, and depth than I will ever begin to know.

I brought two boxes of twelve new Uniball pens with me to the woods. As I finished one off, I would flip it into my pit fire where it would lie in the hot ashes for less than 30 seconds and then blaze up brightly, turning the smoldering embers around it into blazing flames. Even the metal clip turned red hot!

There's another message there as I get ready to return home.

Even something old and worn out can still have fire in it—and burn bright with energy.

Go forth! Go forth! Go forth!

On the first of July, when I first arrived in the woods, the light was breaking in the eastern sky by 3:30 a.m. Now, nearly three months later, the stars are as bright on the eastern horizon at 4:30 a.m. as they were when they were straight over my head.

Message? "The world is continually moving! Who you are and what you do with this realization depends, in part, on you! Are you ready to do your part?"

~ ~ ~

Thank you, God, for your early morning, gentle breeze—even if it *is* 40 degrees! It stimulates my pit fire and keeps it very much alive!

Thank you, God, for the gentle breeze of the Holy Spirit that always and forever stimulates my spiritual life and keeps it alive and vital in much the same way.

Ah! A gentle breeze does so much for a smoldering fire!

Oh! The winds of the Spirit do so much for people and church!

~ ~ ~

A good friend of mine was a star football player for the University of Oklahoma back during the glory days of Coach Charles Burnham "Bud" Wilkinson. Wilkinson served as the head football coach there from 1947 to 1963, leading his Oklahoma Sooners to win three national championships and 14 conference titles. My friend even has a picture of himself carrying Coach Wilkinson on his shoulders after one of those national titles.

Another friend who was also a huge OU Alum (he built some of their fine buildings on the OU campus) often flew the two of them (they both retained season tickets to OU football games) to the weekly OU games in his private jet. I marveled when I heard my friend say one day, "It sure is nice to get in that plane and be in Norman in 20 minutes. The world is moving fast!"

Morning after morning, as I sit in my chair by my pit fire, at times in total darkness and sometimes in the light of day, I see a small, bright light in the distant east.

Is that a star? A planet? A plane? I wondered when I first noticed it.

Time eventually revealed that this was most often a plane carrying troops returning from Afghanistan, stopping at the Bangor Airport to refuel. And sometimes, it was a plane stopping at Bangor to refuel before carrying troops *to* Afghanistan. As it turned out, I was right in the flight path, so I heard and saw these planes regularly.

I later learned that the US military veterans who live in Bangor will not miss a flight into *or* out of their airport. They are always out there, day or night, to greet the incoming or outgoing soldiers. What faithful, faithful service and respect for these people who are giving so much for us all. I was humbled by that awareness.

A now familiar voice within me posed the question: "Larry, are you doing the same for those who have given so much in time and money to the church? Is the church doing the same?"

A worthy thought to ponder!

Greeters for soldiers, coming or going

~ ~ ~

I guess that seventy-five to eighty-five days of my ninety-day stay I had a live fire, usually in a pit, and if it was raining, indoors in that wonderful old wood stove.

So, building my fire and sitting beside it was the center of my day, nearly every day. The insights for my life, church life, church leadership, and "Being God's people in the world" that came to me as I sat with my fire are endless. I captured as many as I could, trusting that the important ones would remain in my memory long enough to get down on paper.

With an alive, vital fire burning brightly—or burning with red-and-white-hot coals, proved to be the very heart of my wilderness wonderings!

~ ~ ~

From time to time, I would collect embers not totally burned—pieces of bark, twigs from branches, needles that fell constantly from the trees around the outer perimeter of the fire pit. These could become fire hazards to spread fire into the forest, especially when woods were as dry as they were early in my stay.

So, periodically, I would gather up these hazards, by rake or by hand, and place them on top of my fire.

Do you know what happens when you do that?

When I load all this debris up on the top of my fire structure, it looks like I have nearly put my fire out.

Then something interesting happens.

Peace and patience and gentle breezes start whittling away at the outer edges of the new burden.

Then heavy smoke begins to rise from the top of the damp, burnt remains I've placed on top of my previously healthy fire.

Slowly, the breeze and the building heat below begin to ignite my additions to the pile—and the wood closest to the pile.

Eventually, the added pile is gone, and my beautifully burning fire reappears!

The odd parallels to the church are plentiful here!

Old, tired, dead embers can be resurrected to contribute to the whole.

The smothering debris reignites the main fire.

Some of the debris really contributes to the fire.

Some of the debris kills out the fire.

Eventually, the debris disappears and is no more. This is life.

Who in our church does each? What is my contribution to each outcome? Did I contribute—or did I kill?

~ ~ ~

I start each day with gratitude and a question: "God, you have gifted me with a new day, and I am deeply grateful. What am I to learn today?"

Today the answer came quickly: "Be aware of the stillness and let the wind blow where it will!"

CHAPTER 19

"Larry! I've done fires for fourteen-and-a-half-billion years. Let me handle it!"

'm nearing the end of my stay here. It's Wednesday of my last week, and my good wood supply is running low. The owner has been so generous in keeping me in wood, I did not wish to ask for more. After all, he gave me this cabin for five weeks (they usually only rent it out for two weeks at a time because of demand) at less than half what they normally charge.

So, I am retrieving wood now to make it last until my last day. As I did so, I had a real battle inside me to, "add wood, add wood, add wood! The fire is dying!"

Deep inside, I kept getting the message,

"Larry, Laaaaaarrrrryyy. I've done fires for fourteen-and-a-half-billion years. Let me handle it!"

So, then I'd look at my fire. Very few flames. However, I noticed that what flames were there were basically blue flame—very hot! So, I sat for a spell and had this same conversation over and over.

"What am I to learn today?"

"Listen to the silence and let the wind blow where it will," which I interpreted to mean: "Stop trying to control your life, Larry. Wait for signals from me!"

So, my battle was between selfish control—and surrender.

Surrender! I don't like that word.

And yet, isn't it the key to an abundant life in Christ?

But there is another dimension here. I did leave the fire alone. I watched the flames' colors. When the blue was gone and yellow-orange flames were low, I knew the fire was dying, and it would die without my adding more wood to it.

Timing is God's work. This is key. Be patient and watch for signs. Go into action when God-directed intuition says, "Act! Go into the world!"

But there's another question here. How do I know whether my intuition is driven by God or by me?

A critical question to answer!

~ ~ ~

I awakened this morning with Willie Nelson's rendition of "When We All Get to Heaven (What A Day of Rejoicing that Will Be!)" running through my mind.

An hour or so later, with the Ol' Willie (Willie Nelson) version of that old hymn still playing in my head, it hit me, "That time is right now, Larry! Celebrate!"

I sat by my early morning fire, watching the morning, another new day's dawn, unfold in brilliant varieties of indescribable color. All I could do was sit in silence, watch, and say, over and over, "Oh Lord, Our God, HOW magnificent!"

~ ~ ~

Every morning for three months, there has been a different and fascinating sky and cloud formation!

What does this say about my life?

I sit by my pit fire today, gazing to the sky above me where high, white, wavy cereus clouds moved lazily from west to east. A lovely songbird, with a song much like a canary, sings her soul out in a high soprano pitch. Between verses of the song there was silence, stillness, peace, and grace!

God, how do I assimilate into my body, my mind, my spirit, and my soul the wonder, the grandeur, and the mystery of your natural world?

And as I finish this line, a duet begins. It is the same type of bird—one on my left and one on my right—harmonizing in their early morning praise to their creator!

≈ ≈ ≈

From out of my deepest memory comes another refrain, this time from a youth camp I once attended:

"Oh, I'll be somewhere, I'll be somewhere, listening for my Lord!"

May this be a mantra for my life!

I *hear* this sweet message with new ears.

I *feel* the message with new determination and intent.

≈ ≈ ≈

Early one morning, as dawn was just beginning, I heard the wind moving in the trees. After looking several times, I still could not tell the direction the wind was blowing the treetops.

The winds of life parallel. We hear or intuit them, and yet we do not know where the wind comes from or where it's going. We just have to act on faith.

Often, when we look back, we can see or recognize the wisdom, plan, or process that was completely out of our awareness at the time.

Was this providence? Predestination? Freedom?

≈ ≈ ≈

It is amazing to me what one small piece of wood can do to activate an entire fire.

Is anyone unimportant?

Every piece of wood burns differently to create a variety of effects, patterns, and heat. Placing one piece of wood in a fire can activate it in a way that you will never see or know unless that one piece is put in there.

Does that say that everyone is important? Does that mean that without a single, specific piece of wood, the whole fire is changed, not as it would have been, had that piece not been added?

I do think this parable of how every log added to a fire *changes* that fire is a good illustration of how we live our lives. There are people and experiences that come and go, and all of those are part of what shapes us to be who we are, how we understand ourselves to be. And every single person in our life changes what our experience of life is all about.

One message I kept hearing over and over: "Larry, you have no future. You have only NOW! The eternal NOW!"

CHAPTER 20

Getting still, all alone

What did I find in the woods?

A much lower stress level, for one thing. For several years now, when I went for my semi-annual medical exam, the doctor would say, "I am putting you on X medication."

I'd say, "Doc, what is that for?"

"Stress!" he'd say.

In my head I'd retort, "I'm semi-retired! I don't have any stress!"

It finally got to the place where my stress level was moving me into depression, and he prescribed an antidepressant. That was a real wake-up call.

So, one purpose for my sabbatical in the woods was to address this issue. Up here, with no appointments, no board meetings, no staff meetings, etc.—just the woods and me and stillness—I became more aware of the many ways I was habitually stressing myself and had no idea I was doing it.

To begin to address this habit, I first created some mantras to use throughout each day to keep me focused on peace, peace, peace, and stillness, *inside* my body. The stillness of the wilderness helped me immensely with this. For a great deal of the time in the wilderness there is very little, if any, sound. The quiet is pervasive and restorative.

I started preaching every Sunday in my own appointment in 1951. Countless times I have said during a worship service, "Be still and know that I am God."

Posted above the doorway to the main room of our home, where we can see it every time we enter, is the familiar passage: "Be still, and know that I am God. I am exalted among the nations, I am exalted in the earth!" (Psalm 46:10 RSV)

"Be still and know that I am God.

I am exalted among the nations,

I am exalted in the earth!"

After all these years of saying, seeing, and repeating this verse, I did not *begin* to know what that scripture meant until I got into real stillness, day and night, day and night, all alone, with no other responsibilities than just to listen to the depths of my soul. Listen, listen, listen, and learn what it really means to "Be still, and know that I am God."

Biggie for me.

I want action! I want to see things done! I have so much to do! Yes, I have always taken time daily to be still—or so I thought. What I discovered was that the deeper I went into the stillness, the deeper and clearer the insights of scripture. And creativity flowed so fast I was literally unable to record it all.

In the wilderness I discovered a whole world of awareness. It has always been inside me—I just didn't have the patience to stop, be still, listen, and learn.

I can go on here with illustrations of this new awareness, but that isn't as important as finding time in our spiritual practices to *just be still.*

So, I consider my three months alone as a basic 101 college class, taught by the Source of all Knowledge, always and forever available to any person.

~ ~ ~

Another ongoing lesson and opportunity for reflection lay in the beauty, grandeur, harmony, and oneness of natural life:

- the ecology of the forest—decay and resurrection,
- the "music of the spheres"—birds, loons, geese, ducks, grand squirrels, chipmunks (and their wars), mice, and my accommodations to them,
- the animal lessons I learned—be friends to all, including the above-listed animals plus Charlie, the Australian shepherd who had no concept of *stranger*,
- the Cosmos—what I could see of it with bare eyes—is infinitesimal,
- the unfolding dawn—the gift of every new day—with the sky painted in the colors of sunrise, still meaningful even after three months in the woods,
- the daily movement of the clouds, unique and everchanging, and
- the crisp clarity of total sunlight, the moody changes in cloud cover, and the multi-sensory joy of rain hitting leaves and dry soil—there is beauty in it all!

How do we humans fit into this total cycle of all of life?

So temporal! So eternal!

There is such wonder and mystery I can hardly contemplate it.

~ ~ ~

Another source of great reflection surrounds the ingenuity and determination of humans and their machines. From taking 90 men all winter to harvest wood, to seven men, with machines, to harvest the same amount of wood, cleaned and cut to fifty-foot lengths, ready to haul in a single day, is a wonder. Trucks that can carry 100,000 pounds of logs with such ease is a wonder.

Nevertheless, it is hardy, harsh work, even now. Snow still gets in their clothes, and there are still subzero temperatures to deal with. There is still a certain amount of suffering with this work—frozen hands and feet—and wrecked bodies from trucks, skidders, and heavy equipment. The pests also remain—mosquitoes, black flies, deer flies. The costs and supply challenges are substantial, even in our time. Skidders are about $200,000 a pop, so these local loggers have gone from operating about 5,000 skidders to less than 1,000—and now they can't buy one except by special order, with only about 2,000 available. The machinery for one harvest crew costs $1.5 to $2 million.

Who can afford it? They're all custom harvesters!

The trappings of ingenuity—amazing machinery

~ ~ ~

I found out that to the very last day—even after ninety days in stillness—I was still habitually doing things with my body, with my mind, to stress myself inappropriately.

How deep does this habit go inside me?
How long will it take to "be still"—and recondition my mind and body to this stillness?
Can I continue to work on this in the hustle and bustle of city life and my day-to-day responsibilities?

~ ~ ~

I have learned something else I have yet to resolve. One angle of all this reflection I am very interested to know more about is: What is *essential* to enabling people to live with unconditional love and peace?

I had a lot of contact with the "unchurched" couple (Jack and Jaime) from my earlier insight for most of my time in the woods. They seemed happier than I assume are many church members. And yet:

- They have no faith of a formal nature.
- They're not married—an anathema to Christians. ("You must marry!")
- They have no active religious practice.
- They seem to have it anyway!

A very important part of this question, something I have put serious thought into here in the woods, is *do I want to stay in the church?*

There are many ways to analyze the church and have been since its inception. It's almost a farce. For centuries "the church" was just a tool of the state. It has and still does have some atrocious practices, right down to United Methodism!

How much of United Methodism's mission today is focused on "What is God's call for this church today?" Are we just maintaining?

When we take an honest look and answer that serious question, isn't that the very issue that holds us back from being what God wants the church to be?

What if *all* churches could discuss this question openly?

Another way of looking at the church, in my own perception, is as an immense gift to the world. Look at its missions of mercy! Consider its educational impact, both culturally and privately. Weigh the effect it has had on the general mores of society.

How can we measure the church's value?

So, after all this reflection and consideration, my take is to stay with the church. There is more positive than negative there, from my perspective. We are doing God's mission adequately, I think, with the circumstances we must work under. We also have a long way to go.

And still, I have a strong conviction of hope and a deep belief in resurrection. I believe when I and others are obedient and faithful to one call, renewal will happen.

It has taken 14.5 billion years for this world to evolve from a ball of fire to creatures like you and me to come into existence with the capabilities and potential to do what we can do! In this big-picture context, the church has been here only a day or two. Let's give it time to evolve, as everything else has!

So, right now, I am committed to staying and seeing what I or we can do to fulfill The Great Commission, which is the instruction of the resurrected Jesus Christ to his disciples to spread the gospel to all the nations of the world.

CHAPTER 21

Whispers of prevenient grace

now have a new understanding of and appreciation for Wesley's idea of prevenient grace. John Wesley described one aspect of God's grace as *prevenience*, or "preventing" grace. Prevenient grace is present in all creation—in the natural order, in human consciousness, and in the relationships and heritage into which we are born.

Prevenient grace, according to Wesley, comes from the divine image of God within each of us, that enlightens everyone who comes into the world "to do justice, and to love kindness, and to walk humbly with your God?" (Micah 6:8 RSV), —the pull toward a shared vision of what can be. Even considering human sin and brokenness, Wesley believed that God's prevenient grace prevents the destruction of that divine image within each of us. Wesley also compared God's grace to a journey in which the map to be followed are all gifts. The landscape encountered, the mind and eyes that conceived and perceived the journey, and even the explorer who blazed the trail ahead of us are all parts of this gift of Divine grace.

In considering my own journey, both the physical journey to the North Maine Woods and the spiritual journey of spending three months alone with my creator, prevenient grace became very real to me. So much more than the concept I thought I understood in all my years of ministry. My, how I learned—had to learn—of this Divine grace firsthand during my time in the woods.

I had to move three times, with very little notice each time. And every move proved to be an even better, more scenic setting! How does this happen? Then, after being cut off from my lifeline, two new sources of help and support emerged almost immediately and were there to the end. Did the ease of my finding new openings and solutions on each move happen because I have some kind of special relationship with my Creator? Absolutely not. God shows no partiality. This Divine gift lies, hidden in plain sight within each of us. It is upon to us to do our part to discover it!

So, does faithful religious practice enhance prevenient grace? If we accept that prevenient grace is God's freely-given grace that comes before, without anticipation of human decisions, it is interesting to me to consider my water situation.

When I first arrived in the North Maine Woods, I learned that there was a well, so pure water was available here. But then the well became unavailable, so I got pure water from the spring. Then the spring ran dry. My choice then was to go to town, sixty minutes round trip (and pay someone for this). Then appeared the unanticipated opportunity to move to Porter Point, where there was an endless supply of water purified from Nicatous Lake, one of the largest lakes in Maine. Plenty of water, just fifty feet from camp.

Is this prevenient grace?

Another dimension to prevenient grace is I did not recognize it as it was being given. Only upon reflection did I see it. Was this because of my lack of awareness? Then came my answer: if it is prevenient, no way can I see it as it happens! Prevenient means *before*!

Another example of prevenient grace I feel extremely grateful for is my physical safety in these remote, North Maine Woods for three full months. I did not fear the animals, really. The more real fear to me was the forest floor, slick with leaves and pine needles, sloped and dotted with boulders akin to ski-slope moguls.

Every few feet lay a granite rock, ranging in bulk from the size of my hand to large, room-sized boulders. Each threatened my safe navigation. With years of undisturbed leaves and needles all around me, a spot may look safe to step on, but then I would sink into a hole where the water had washed away the soil beneath the floor of the woods.

Anywhere I went in the forest, fallen trees dotted my path, sometimes every few feet. When trees lose branches—knocked off by wind or wild animals, these broken tree branches leave sharp, jagged hardwood points. Any fall could be lethal, and with my limited balance I was at risk daily for a major back, head, lung, or limb injury from a fall in those woods.

I have fallen a great deal during my time here, and probably had more close calls to major injury than I even realized. And yet I escaped any harm. I can only see this as prevenient grace.

~ ~ ~

There is an experience I still do not know how to put into words. I sense it cannot be put into words.

When "The word became flesh" (John 1:14 RSV) in Christ, is this the big bang? (I think the two are synonymous. I think the word became flesh *in* the big bang.) And the question is, did we *all* become flesh in "the big bang?" Aren't we all part of that same Divine spark? This is the best way I know how to say it.

Paradoxes are easily accepted, and I ran into a host of these during my time in the woods. I would write a thought or insight, and before even finishing it, I'd see a paradoxical reality that is just as true.

Isn't God a paradox? God can be in the present now in my life, but I cannot define what God is.

Here in the woods, mental contradictions seem to melt away. Forgiving, letting go, loving at different levels—all seem as rational as breathing. There is no need to "try hard" to do these things. They happen with a new ease.

I think a lot of people are out there "trying hard," and they need to just let go and accept what *is*. To me, a person who "tries hard" will never get there.

"There is only Christ, he is everything, and he is in everything," Paul said, "Here there cannot be Greek and Jew, circumcised and uncircumcised, barbarian, Scyth'ian, slave, free man, but Christ is all, and in all." (Colossians 3:11 RSV)

In his December 6, 2018 Daily Meditation "Christ is Everywhere," Father Richard Rohr adds his own insight: "This is not pantheism; it is the much more subtle and subversive pan*en*theism, or God *in* all things."

This reality seems to be what Paul calls "the mind of Christ." (Philippians 2:5 RSV) How do you put the experience of this truth into words?

You cannot!

CHAPTER 22

Idyllic setting, etched in my gratitude

A s I sit by my final pit fire this morning, I contemplate my return home from three months of solitude in Maine. I stop this mental meandering from time to time to just look up and all around me, trying to memorize every detail of this idyllic setting. I am overcome with gratitude for this time, this experience, this fresh immersion in my relationship with God.

In a way I don't want my time here to end. In another way, which began as a faint inkling and is now growing steadily toward excitement, I want to see what I can hold onto from this time. I am not idealistic enough to think I can hold onto it all.

Some of it will—and naturally should—slip away once I return to my life in Fort Worth. I won't, for example, be compelled to do my daily walk for water and wood. I won't have to actively seek out company and companionship. And among the best of these, indoor plumbing will make my personal business and hygiene much more manageable.

But there are other things I do want to keep. Some of them may take some work but will nonetheless be worth it. Especially because now I have been shown and have experienced the difference between what I thought I knew about the value of silence and stillness and the active daily practice of it.

One thing the woods taught me to feel most deeply is how much more responsibility I have for my life than I have believed all my life. I was raised saturated in "God must do it! You are a worm!" (See the "For such a worm as I" line from the hymn "Amazing Grace.") I was taught that this was to be interpreted and practiced as, "Be passive. Let God do it all."

I return from my time in Maine with a new understanding: "Allow God to do it *through* me." I feel like I have been put in charge of my life. I decided to take absolute and full responsibility.

The very vital and most important key to living into this new understanding? Live in what Richard Rohr calls the "Naked Now," meaning *moment by moment*. Keep the hot coal, powerful flames of silence and stillness in my awareness ("Be still, and know that I am God"), and God will naturally, appropriately, and at the right time, act in and through me. I may not see it or feel it until it is in process—or even finished—but knowing that there is always a hand of prevenient grace at the center and bottom line is a new awareness for me.

Closely related to this whole idea of "I am in charge of my life" is the implication that I will more efficiently play this out through intentional self-care of my physical body, my mental habits, and my spiritual practices.

So, understanding that I am totally responsible for every choice or decision I make, I am also aware that there is a prevenient grace running beneath and gifting it all!

Another paradox?

~ ~ ~

In my vocation as a counselor, through my years of training, personal experience, and what I witnessed in others' lives, I've seen again and again how very destructive and unhealthy stress can be. I intentionally tried to address this issue in myself for many years. Surprisingly, even upon semi-retirement, lowering my stress was still a central issue for me.

I think I made progress in these woods, but I did not win this war! It was in Maine, focusing day after day on the Psalmist's words and asking, "what did you mean by 'lead me beside still waters?'" Eventually I began to see *how* "He restores my soul." (Psalm 23:3 RSV)

"Be *still*, and *know* that I am God." (Psalm 46:10 RSV)

I did this work in a sanctuary of solitude. No distractions. No schedule to keep. No responsibility except to maximize my opportunity to learn all I could about life, about Larry, and about what we call God!

There was a deafening stillness, an absence of noise, through most of each day. And, when the silence was interrupted, it was by the song of praise from a bird or the natural chuckle of a small animal.

In the stillness of these woods I finally stopped, changed, and retooled myself to become peaceful and still inside, down to my innermost core. Here in this divine sanctuary, I have built new strategies, established some new patterns. I'm committed, as my priority, to maintain this state of inner being even in the rush and push of the city. In the setting of being on a church staff, I am committed. In the setting of home, wife, and self, I am committed!

Can I do it?

I think I can.

Will I do it?

Time will tell.

Could I have reached this state of quietness inside without Maine, without three months of stillness?

I can only say I never did, until now.

I suspect the Psalmist is right. We can only find this peace that lives deep in our core, the peace where we are meant and created to live, when we immerse ourselves in a setting of extended stillness!

It was expensive to do this—much more than I thought it would cost at the beginning. By prevenient grace I had a couple of wonderful friends to help me, a wife who is a superb manager of money to partner with me, and a senior pastor who gifted me with the time and opportunity to do it.

Had I known it would cost this much to do it, would I have done it?

Probably not.

Was it worth it?

Absolutely, beyond any question in my mind. As I see it, prevenient grace made it happen, and I am beyond grateful!

In addition to the deep inner peace that has all but eliminated the stress I carry in my body, I return from the wilderness with a wonderful new energy, an inner vitality that buoys me into and through each day with joy and excitement!

~ ~ ~

I find rare clarity and direction for God-centered living via Paramahansa Yogananda (1893-1952), an Indian Hindu monk, yogi, and guru who introduced millions to the teachings of meditation and yoga. He was one of those rare, enlightened persons from India who did an exquisite job of melding Hindu and Christian religious ideas in America in the early twentieth century—exactly what Karen Armstrong did in the early 21st century.

Armstrong, considered to be one of the world's leading thinkers on religion and spirituality, is a former Catholic nun who has since described herself as a "freelance monotheist." Her book *A History of God* (Knopf, 1993) is another of my favorite examples of bringing multiple established religious traditions together in harmony with the idea to live by compassion.

Here is Paramahansa Yogananda's perspective on how humans first found God: "First you must have a right concept of God—a definite idea through which you can form a relationship with Him—and then you must meditate and pray until that mental conception becomes changed into actual perception. Then you will know Him. If you persist, the Lord will come."

This prescriptive describes precisely what I attempted to do in Maine. Get away from all distractions—meetings, appointments, social contacts—and focus on one thing:

"God, how can I know You?"

Quoting Jesus, Paramahansa Yogananda exclaims: "The Kingdom of God is within you!"

It's not within the Bible, Sunday School class, mission, and outreach (even though these are vital components to living in the Kingdom of God), but "within you!"

"Be still and know that I am God."

"He leads me beside still waters."

We find God in stillness, silence, aloneness—and *within* our inner being. These three months gave me a brief introduction into this world that was new, refreshing, and the beginning, I feel, of transformation.

Then, says Paramahansa Yogananda, "God moves you into action and activity to live and love in the mundane or secular venue of life. It is God, living God's self, in and through us, to the world."

Sound familiar?

> "I have been crucified with Christ; it is no longer I who live, but Christ who lives in me; and the life I now live in the flesh I live by faith in the Son of God, who loved me and gave himself for me." (Galatians 2:20 RSV)

So, Hindus had in essence what Christ had and was, thousands of years before Jesus came on the scene.

Truth is truth. God is God.

Why wouldn't people understand this thousands of years ago—as well as today?

(HAPTER 23

Just . . . be

On my return to Fort Worth after three months in the Maine wilderness, I have reflected on my experiences in a number of ways. One very meaningful idea I have had for considering this time is this.

I have been in a "wilderness behavioral unit" for three months with Christ as my doctor, psychiatrist, and guide.

I was isolated. I was confined. If I got food or water, I had to depend on someone else. I was in a lockdown unit!

I also wanted to talk to Patty on the phone. The telecom companies don't even know there *is* a North Maine Woods.

From 3:00 to 4:00 a.m. each morning until 7:00 to 8:00 p.m. each evening every single day was a series of long, individual counseling sessions with one called Jesus. Now that is quite an honor—to have three months of daily one-on-one time with the Lord of Life!

There was never a dull moment. To my amazement, I never once felt bored. I could not wait to get up in the morning to bed my fire, make my coffee, and sit down for my sessions. I hand-wrote nearly 400 pages of insights. They came faster than I could record them. I'm still recalling some of the creative thoughts I had, and now I am writing them down, too. I got hand cramps from writing. I took a fresh box of twelve black pens to write with and ran out while I was there.

I had no responsibility to anyone except Larry Grubb and my Creator. No appointments, no board meetings, committee meetings, staff meetings, or family time. Just me and my Creator!

That provided a lot of time to think, reflect, problem solve, and just BE.

DO absolutely nothing.

SIT STILL in God's sanctuary of mystery and wonder and just LISTEN for a fresh word—of praise, of love, and sometimes of judgment that really made me squirm.

How cathartic! How therapeutic! How healing! How inspiring—and how uncomfortable, at times, as God takes me to the woodshed!

God is love. And love has to be tough at times. Our Father in heaven knows how to use *all* of love's strategies to teach, inform, nurture, comfort, and protect!

I returned to the real world feeling cleansed and healed, physically, spiritually, and emotionally. I have a new and different sense of who and what I am. I'm much more at peace. I feel comfortable in my skin in a way I don't ever recall experiencing in my past. I feel I have found the pot of gold at the end of the rainbow, the pearl of great price.

I also feel like I am in kindergarten, just learning how to be me. I feel a new peace, freedom, and contentment that is fresh and exhilarating. I feel a deep joy of anticipation to go forth and answer these simple questions:

"Larry, can you keep it? Can you grow it? Can you mature it?"

I don't know. I am committed to giving it my best shot. I believe God created us to live, learn, and be in a world of the secular, the mundane, and the simple. Jesus did it. I feel he calls you and me to do it.

I feel honored! I feel humble! I feel blessed! I feel deeply grateful and indebted to everyone in my life who did their part to allow me this holy privilege.

Here is the lightest and briefest summary of what this unique experience meant to me:

"Teach us, O Lord, what it means to be still! When You said, 'I will lead you beside still waters' and 'I will restore your soul,' what did You have in mind?"

"Be still, be still, be *still* and know that I am God!"

Upon my return I have learned that the beat of my heart is a continual reminder that God is at work.

Listen.

Take direction of how to live each moment.

This is living by *being*.

~ ~ ~

Lao-Tzu was a prophet who was the keeper of the imperial archive in the ancient capital of China, Luoyang, 2,500 years ago. Seeing the decay of his culture during a time of much war and chaos, he decided to ride westward, into the desert.

At Hangu Pass, a gatekeeper named Yin His, knowing of Lao-Tzu's reputation as a man of wisdom, begged him to record his wisdom. This was the birth of the *Tao Te Ching*, written in 5,000 Chinese characters.

In the forty-fifth verse of the Tao, 2,500 years ago, Lao-Tzu records, "Stillness and tranquility set things in order in the universe."

Living in a culture of blaring sirens, loud train whistles, constant city noise, and the sound of roaring jets, I don't have much real stillness in my life.

So, I headed east instead of west, for 90 days alone in the wilderness—the North Maine Woods—to explore these words of Lao-Tzu alongside the tenth verse of Psalm 46, written 3,000 to 3,500 years ago: "Be still, and know that I am God. I am exalted among the nations, I am exalted in the earth!" (Psalm 46:10 RSV)

In our culture today, it is *also* a time of war and chaos in nearly every area of life, including the Body of Christ, the Church.

Something needs to give.

And I felt I would not know what or know how until I got Larry Grubb straight on some things. Like Lao-Tzu, I retreated to stillness. No wheels, no communication, no electricity, no running water. Only stillness and God's magnificent wilderness sanctuary.

In *Change Your Thoughts - Change Your Life,* Dr. Wayne Dyer theorizes that if Lao-Tzu were alive today he'd probably say something like: "Stop chasing your dreams." Dyer expounds even further on this idea, adding: "Allow them to come to you in perfect order with unquestioned timing. Slow down your frantic pace and practice being hollow like the cave and open to all possibilities like the uncarved wood. Make stillness a regular part of your daily practice. Imagine all that you'd like to experience in life and then let go. Trust the Tao to work in divine perfection, as it does with everything on the planet. You don't really need to rush or force anything. Be an observer and receiver rather than the pushy director of your life. It is through this unhurried unfolding that you master your existence in the way of the Tao."

The path before me

One of history's great mystical thinkers, Meister Eckhart (1260 - 1327), a German theologian, philosopher, and speculative mystic whose experiences and practical spiritual philosophy of seeing God in all, poetically put it this way, several centuries ago:

"Every object, every creature, every man, woman, child
Has a soul and it is the destiny of all,
To see as God sees, to know as God knows,
To feel as God feels, to be
As God
Is."

Do we not need stillness to do this? The wisdom of our past says, "Yes."

I am moving to a place that says stillness is the only way to truly know God!

Or, as the 13th century mystical poet, Rumi, a citizen of Iraq, sums up what God may be calling us to know:

"You are the truth from foot to brow. Now, what else would you like to know?"

Upon my return, in my scripture and devotional reading I see with new eyes, hear with new ears, understand with fresh and vital insights. My life has a different foundation. My mission has broadened and sharpened. My vitality and energy are much improved.

≈ ≈ ≈

Upon returning, I sense a new unity in all of life, rather than the Aristotelian dualistic mind our culture, education, and life are all grounded on. I was raised in a culture that says, "It needs to be logical—rational. There is a right way and a wrong way."

I see paradox, paradox, paradox! Nearly everything I see, hear, believe, has a paradoxical dimension. I see all truth as paradox.

I believe this is what Jesus taught in the beatitudes.

The Eight Beatitudes*
(*Followed by "Larry's Wilderness Beatitudes")

Blessed are the poor in spirit, for theirs is the kingdom of heaven.

I had to feel poor in spirit to go to Maine. Could God take care of me in this setting—no car, phone, minimal communication with the outside world? I did find the kingdom of heaven in this environment; God did abundantly care for me.

Blessed are those who mourn, for they shall be comforted.

Mourning could be present for one who is alone in the wilderness. To my amazement, I felt comfort, peace, and acceptance.

Blessed are the meek, for they shall inherit the earth.

I felt meek, uncertain, and questioning as I chose to move into the wilderness. At the same time, I felt hopeful and confident that I would be OK. A true paradox.

Blessed are those who hunger and thirst for righteousness, for they shall be filled.

I went into the wilderness hungry and thirsty. I did not know what lay ahead. I saw death as a possibility. Surely Patty had this thought, too, and yet she trusted me to go. I ended up truly filled by this experience and could have gone longer if that had been a possibility.

Blessed are the merciful, for they shall obtain mercy.

What I learned in the wilderness is patience, kindness, and mercy. They all speak to the same thing. In experiencing God's mercy in the wilderness, I chose to reflect this trait in my living. I lived with wild beasts that could have killed me. To reflect on this is to know and accept mercy in daily living.

Blessed are pure in heart, for they shall see God.

I could live with faith and trust in the wilderness and learn more clearly what it means to be pure in heart. I never saw myself as pure in heart, yet the wilderness invited me to consider what this might mean. Pure in heart can be living in perfection. To me this is impossible. If it means having the intent to be pure in heart, maybe this is attainable. It is an honorable goal.

Blessed are the peacemakers, for they shall be called children of God.

I think all Christians are called to be peacemakers. The wilderness is a good place to practice peacemaking, because I am where other responsibilities cannot push me, and I can focus on the call to be peaceful as a person. I can't be a peacemaker until I am at peace as a person.

Blessed are they which are persecuted for righteousness' sake, for theirs is the kingdom of heaven.
This is not my case in the wilderness, so I can only imagine what this might be like. I think of my brave mothers and fathers in early Christian times who were living under the oppression of violent Rome. Christians were fed to hungry lions, and many were hung alive to die on a cross. What terrible punishment for being righteous! They did it gladly, though, knowing the kingdom of heaven was theirs.

~ ~ ~

I went to Maine to study the emerging church culture. I wasn't there long before I realized that I had the wrong agenda.

This event was about an an emerging Larry—not an emerging church. If church is to be different, Larry Grubb must be different.

Words that have haunted me for a long time, came from this insight of Albert Einstein: "Our problem in society is not, 'how do we change bad people.' It is all about good people who see something that needs to change and does nothing."

That stings. (It ought to sting.)

So *that* became my focus in Maine.

One evolving idea that came out of the experience was, if God can guide the planets that twist around the sun so perfectly, can I not trust that same Source to fully (not partially or conveniently) direct my life?

~ ~ ~

500 years ago, Kabir, one of India's revered poets, made this pithy observation:

Observation: "The fish in the water that is thirsty needs serious professional counseling."

I resonate deeply with this description of me—and how often I want more knowledge, more wisdom, more acceptance, and more "things," the hallmark of our culture today.

Three months in Maine was a refreshing reminder from our Source: "Larry, reality is not in things you learn or possess. It is in recognizing who I created you to BE. Practice more giving away and see what unexpected joy and satisfaction you naturally feel."

Jesus put it this way: "Give and it will be given to you. A good measure, pressed down, shaken together, running over, will be put into your lap, for the measure you give will be the measure you get back." (Luke 6:38 RSV)

I am accepting of others, with their limitations and imperfections, as I do the same for myself.

It works in reverse.

CHAPTER 24

A heightened experience of being alive

n the program, "Joseph Campbell and the Power of Myth with Bill Moyers," which is a timeless 1988 PBS documentary series featuring conversations between mythologist Joseph Campbell and journalist Bill Moyers exploring the classic hero cycle and enduring hero patterns in literature and life, Campbell encourages his audience to view parts of their own lives as "heroic journeys."

"People say that what we're all seeking is a meaning for life," he says. "I don't think that is what we are really seeking. I think that what we are seeking is an experience of being alive, so that our life experiences on the purely physical plane will have resonance within our innermost being and reality, so that we actually *feel* the rapture (excitement and joy) of being alive."

Arriving back in Fort Worth after my own "hero's journey" into stillness in the remote North Maine Woods, I feel so much more alive, excited, and motivated.

I look at my bookshelves and see hosts of books I want to read *right now*.

I look at the scores of old, antique clocks stored in my barn and think, "I want to rebuild and get those pieces of history back into circulation."

I look at my list of homebound church members (Saints!) and feel the urge to go see them *now*.

I see small tasks about my house and yard, and I do them now, with a new eagerness and joy, whereas before I'd say, "I will do that later."

This same theme of immediacy and aliveness permeates my whole life.

≈ ≈ ≈

I came to see with clarity that I am a spiritual being having a temporal experience, *not* a physical being having a spiritual experience. I went to Maine thinking the latter. I returned with a deep knowing that death won't touch who I really am or who we all really are.

Much has been written about this (the book, *You Are a Spiritual Being Having a Human Experience* by Bob Frissell comes to mind), and I think it is worth remembering and revisiting this whenever our human experience gets to be just too much, and we wonder, "Why is this happening?" The truth is we may never know, but everything that happens is part of our soul's human journey. I'm not sure how much that helps in times of extreme stress, but somehow, coming back to this great truth settles me.

Move into the joy and delight of experiencing genuine eternity right now, in this moment!

≈ ≈ ≈

Big question: "Can I carry the peace, harmony, joy of living in the wilderness into the noise, chaos, pressure, stress, and demand of urban life?"

I am finding it possible, and it takes intentional practice for it to become a natural way of living: "Peace I leave with you; my peace I give to you; not as the world gives do I give to you. Let not your hearts be troubled, neither let them be afraid." (John 14:27 RSV)

Paramahansa Yogananda, one of India's wonderful gurus who believed in the truth of Jesus, challenged Americans at the beginning of the twentieth century with this idea: "The mind is a switchboard which we control. Learn to turn off the five senses, meditate, and contemplate in stillness, and God will meet us in fresh and vital ways. As we learn to do this, we tune out stress and chaos in our life and replace it with peace and relaxation."

I bring peace into my personal chaos by reading devotional books and scripture every day, and then I sit in silence to think about them. In the morning when I get up, sometimes before breakfast, and sometimes after breakfast, I do this and just try to be quiet and listen to what I read in the scripture and in the devotional. This is something I learned from my dad, and so I have just continued that because I found it to be a useful exercise. It is helpful for me.

~ ~ ~

My incognito, post-sabbatical return to church

Spending three months alone in the wilderness meant I was mostly *alone* with my thoughts and observations, except for my occasional human contact on a walk or getting food and water. It seemed that when I needed human contact, God reached out to me in the form of a variety of newly found friends I didn't even realize were sharing those woods with me, each having their own experience in their own time of self-discovery.

Did I get lonely? No.

And, I will readily admit, walking back into my home church sanctuary for the first time was a deep comfort and a wonderful feeling of warmth and acceptance. It had an infinite, sacred quality to it.

I came back to church incognito, as a person who is homeless, and I felt at home in a community of loving, accepting, caring people. They didn't know me. I did know them!

Take this a step deeper. We don't know God. Oh, we are grandiose enough to think we do from time to time.

It is an illusion.

However, God *does* know us. Matthew 10:30 RSV tells us *"the hairs of your head are all numbered"* (for some of us this number is far lower than for others!), to assure us of our individual value to God, the Source of life.

We were created by this Source of life. We are sustained by this Source of life in *every breath* we take. Our intimate, hidden, vital connection to this Source is present in every moment.

Stillness, aloneness, and quietness enable us to develop new recognition of our Source and our need for a relationship with it. There is a real and practical *friendship* to be had in that stillness for each and every one of us. And we only find this relationship *in* stillness.

There is also a sense of returning home in this stillness. And the deeper we go, the more real, personal, and joyful this relationship becomes. There is no limit, no end, or ultimate knowing. It grows forever when we invite it, in this life and beyond!

I heard about the Holy Land all my life and had never been there. I knew it only through others who had been there and what I imagined in my reading about it. Then, in 1992 I went there for 10 days. Only then did the Holy Land become personal, real, and alive to me.

So, in *this* holy journey with the Divine, it is one thing for others to tell us about it; it is very different when we arrive and find it for ourselves in the stillness!

~ ~ ~

Are you tired, with low energy and even lower, motivation? Try quiet and stillness as an intervention.

This was one astonishing outcome of my time in the wilderness.

Now I see things I *want* to do.

I am motivated to do things now that I had lost interest in.

I have natural energy to do so much more, i.e., exercise, hobbies, time with Patty.

I returned with a strong desire to spend more time with friends—deep, quality, significant time.

I find a new emotional sensitivity to others that was dull and lacking before.

Stillness permeates our whole being and energizes us for being God's persona in our world. There is joy and excitement in every new day—as it unfolds and as it progresses.

Realize and flow in that infinite, eternal, powerful, and quiet river of love we call God.

The Presence!

The Now!

Truly *live* each moment!

~ ~ ~

Another thing I am noticing immediately upon my return home is how I am experiencing a more natural loving, kindness, and compassion for myself and for others.

I walk early in the mornings. I have a neighbor who walks or jogs every morning. We nearly always meet two or three times a morning. Some days she speaks; some days she won't speak. In the past this would evoke feelings of judgment, shame or anger in me.

Upon returning from Maine, I offer a simple prayer for her as I start my walk, encounter, and separate from her. I speak, regardless of how she responds. She has a right to not speak to me, even though we have encountered each other on our respective morning exercise paths for years.

I certainly feel better loving and releasing my emotions around these encounters rather than trying to figure out, "Why will she not speak?"

~ ~ ~

In some respects, it is difficult to be precise about how I experience life differently after my time in Maine, but one awareness is becoming much clearer. I feel less of an edge in my being.

Before, I felt a sense of being unsettled; a gnawing, unsettled compulsion to always be about something. Now I feel settled, softer, quieter, and more centered.

~ ~ ~

I feel like I'm finally developing my "third eye." Jesus says in Sermon on the Mount: "The eye is the lamp of the body. So, if your eye is sound, your whole body will be full of light;" (Matthew 6:22 RSV).

In *Man's Eternal Quest*, Paramahansa Yogananda (also the author of *Autobiography of a Yogi*) explores a whole litany of subjects including meditation, life after death, health and healing, and other enigmas of life. For readers he describes as "those who have held within their hearts an uncertain hope about the reality of God, and for seekers who have already turned toward the Supreme in their quest," he explains that intuition, or *direct knowledge*, does not depend on data from the senses. Rather, this knowledge is what we sometimes call the *sixth sense*. He affirms that we *all* have it; some more developed than others.

My take on all this is something we also find in the Gospel of Luke: "For behold, The kingdom of God is within you." (Luke 17:21 KJV).

The kingdom of God is not something we find in church, theology, etc. People may assume that when "the Word became flesh" (John 1:14, RSV), it refers to the physical, human embodiment of God we know as Jesus. It goes much deeper than that. It means that the "Kingdom of God" is not a place. It is God working in and through me and you—*our* flesh and blood. Jesus gave us the ideal, and now we are to follow that example as best we can.

I see this awareness as an extremely important skill to focus upon and develop. In my experience, disregarding this simple wisdom gets me into chaos. And vice versa. Any time I followed this urging and wisdom, my life was enhanced!

The Buddhists also put major focus on this wisdom. They call it *mindfulness* and invite devotees to do everything they do *mindfully*, out of the wisdom and direction of the third eye.

Some 2,500 years ago, in *Tao Te Ching*, Lao-Tzu called following this innate, third-eye wisdom and direction "The Way"—as did early Christians. These "Followers of The Way" followed Jesus' instruction from his Sermon on the Mount and in five different places in John's gospel:

"I and the Father are one." (John 10:30 RSV)

"But if I do them, even though you do not believe me, believe the works, so that you may know and understand that the Father is in me and I am in the Father." (John 10:38 RSV)

"Do you not believe that I am in the Father and the Father in me? The words that I say to you I do not speak on my own authority; but the Father who dwells in me does his works." (John 14:10 RSV)

"And now I am no more in the world, but they are in the world, and I am coming to you. Holy Father, protect them in your name that you have given me, so that they may be one, as we are one." (John 17:11 RSV)

"The glory which thou hast given me I have given to them, that they may be one even as we are one." (John 17:22 RSV)

In his final discourse with his closest friends, Jesus expressed his desire that they all become of one heart and mind: "even as thou, Father, art in me, and I in thee, that they also may be in us, so that the world may believe that thou hast sent me." (John 17:21 RSV)

The key takeaway here for me is that we don't find this oneness/wisdom/third eyesight in our five senses, as impressive as they are. This kind of inner wisdom is a sixth, subtle sense that we must intentionally focus upon, learn from, and grow with.

During my time in the woods, I feel this sense has been sharpened a bit in me. I'm still in kindergarten—an excited kindergartener—focused on this new growth.

CHAPTER 25

Transcendence is attributed to the divine knowledge, as well as being.

return from the North Maine Woods with a much deeper appreciation of the deep spiritual contributions of what the Kahalani, Hindu, Buddhist, Muslim, and Christian faiths offer us. There is much connectivity in all.

Ken Wilber, a contemporary American philosopher, writes about something called *transpersonal psychology*, which integrates within the framework of modern psychology the spiritual and transcendent aspects of the human experience. In its religious connotation, transcendence, or that which goes beyond what we as human beings can legitimately know, refers to the nature and power of God that is beyond all physical laws, a state of being that overcomes and is independent of the limitations of our physical existence. We can experience transcendence in prayer and meditation; and, in many varied religious traditions, transcendence is attributed to the divine as *knowledge* as well as being.

Considering all of this (and much more, of course) Wilber developed his own *integral theory*, or "theory of everything" philosophy to attempt to integrate a wide diversity of theories and human wisdom into one single framework. In drawing together the perspectives of all previous paradigms, including those that appear to contradict one another, into an interrelated network that mutually enrich one another, Wilbur's work sought to encompass the living totality of matter, body, mind, soul, and spirit.

I guess I have always sensed this connectivity, and I remembered some of its underpinnings from my professional life, studies, and experiences. But it wasn't until my time alone, in the stillness of the natural world, that I really felt and understood this deep, universal connectivity Wilbur's integral theory addressed and sought to describe.

~ ~ ~

Maine helped me move my head to my heart in several important ways. Western culture stresses thinking, being logical. If we can't prove it scientifically, it isn't true. Eastern culture stresses our mystical, intuitive, sixth sense. What I've come to understand is this: there is wisdom and learning our five senses simply can't capture.

This is the image of God side of us.

We are created with gifts that we think no other organism has. (This may not be true.) We can think, feel, solve problems, create, and dream. These gifts and how we use them create the person we are. They create the society and the culture in which we live!

So, what is the implication of all this? I think it is that every problem is my problem, too, because I am part of a single organism called *humankind,* a single cell in one body called humanity.

In I Corinthians Paul said, "If one member suffers, all suffer together; if one member is honored, all rejoice together." (I Corinthians 12:26 RSV)

And here's another huge implication of this understanding: What *I* think and feel affects *everyone*. Solving church, family, political, and world problems is up to *me*.

God's message to the world via Christ is, "Go, love, accept, forgive, heal, make whole." And of course, we do have a choice. We can choose instead to fear, hate, get mad, judge, criticize, destroy. Regardless of our choice, individually or collectively, *we are all part of all of it.*

~ ~ ~

"Be very intentional with each moment, Larry. Live in the NOW. Even on workdays."

On Wednesday, I sat at home and wrote what I was feeling God calling me to do, rather than getting out to visit senior church members or going to the office. This was my design in Maine—and how it played out at home!

After my quiet time journaling and listening for God's instruction for my day, I went with a few books to study on post-Christian and postmodern thoughts, including John Wesley's famous quote: "The world is my Parish" that has inspired so many in ministry.

As the founder of Methodism, John Wesley was banned from the pulpit in the Anglican church because his preaching was considered too radical and controversial. This all came about after Wesley's life-changing conversion experience in which his intellectual understanding of faith was transformed into a personal experience during a meeting on Aldersgate Street in 1738 London.

As a priest without a parish, Wesley's ministry then took on a new expression that changed what it meant to minister exclusively to a particular geographic community. This drew criticism from many, even accusations of "trespassing" on other priests' assigned parishes. Hence the source of John Wesley's famous quote, penned in his pivotal June 11, 1739 journal entry: "I look upon all the world as my parish; thus far I mean, that, in whatever part of it I am, [it is my] duty to declare unto all that are willing to hear, the glad tidings of salvation. This is the work which I know God has called me to; and sure I am that his blessing attends it."

~ ~ ~

What does The Great Commission (found in Mark 16:15 RSV) "Go into all the world" have to do with my time in Maine?

Here's what I came up with: The world is not coming *to* us for ministry—it's running *from* us. Thus, my quest. What do we need to do differently in the church? In us? In me?

Christ was global. From my personal one-to-one with family, friends, career, church, community, and world, *I* am global. My reach in ministry is far beyond what I can know. Our "millennials" are also global—they network with people worldwide.

Shortly after arriving in Maine, the first message I got was "change Larry." So, I spent three months listening in stillness and reflecting on all I saw, heard, and felt to do just that. I took all the books I thought I needed to read with me to the woods, and then I inextricably knew that everything I *really* needed to contemplate and absorb was provided for me, there in the stillness of the astounding natural world.

~ ~ ~

"The world is a dangerous place, not because of those who do evil, but because of those who look on and do nothing."

Going back to that famous Albert Einstein quote, my insights came in layers:

- How I am one of "those who look on and do nothing?"

- What am I to do about that?

- What does that mean, in practical, day-to-day terms?

First, I think it means I need to get fire in my belly and be more faithful to my present call. Second, I think it means I need to "be prophetic," accepting what that may cost in terms of loss of job, reduced income, alienation/rejection by others.

This was Jesus' model for us. This is what he meant when he instructed all who would follow him to "take up his cross and follow me." (Matthew 16:24 RSV)

Then a familiar hymn lyric floated into my mind:

"Were you there when they crucified our Lord?"

My answer to this timeless question?

"Yes, and I still am when I fail to speak and act out of love or tough love."

~ ~ ~

In 1 Timothy, Paul talks about being "Commissioned by God."

"I thank him who has given me strength for this, Christ Jesus our Lord, because he judged me faithful by appointing me to his service, though I formerly blasphemed and persecuted and insulted him; but I received mercy because I had acted ignorantly in unbelief, and the grace of our Lord overflowed for me with the faith and love that are in Christ Jesus. The saying is sure and worthy of full acceptance, that Christ Jesus came into the world to save sinners. And I am the foremost of sinners; but I received mercy for this reason, that in me, as the foremost, Jesus Christ might display his perfect patience for an example to those who were to believe in him for eternal life. To the King of ages, immortal, invisible, the only God, be honor and glory for ever and ever. Amen. This charge I commit to you, Timothy, my son, in accordance with the prophetic utterances which pointed to you, that inspired by them you may wage the good warfare, holding faith and a good conscience. By rejecting conscience, certain persons have made shipwreck of their faith, among them Hymenae'us and Alexander, whom I have delivered to Satan that they may learn not to blaspheme." (I Timothy 1:12-20 RSV)

In this passage Paul is trying to get his Galatian churches back on track. As often happened, the old guard had gotten back and moved them back into their old ways:

Immediately after my calling—without consulting anyone around me and without going up to Jerusalem to confer with those who were apostles long before I was—I got away to Arabia. Later I returned to Damascus, but it was three years before I went up to Jerusalem to compare stories with Peter. I was there only fifteen days—but what days they were! Except for our Master's brother James, I saw no other apostles. (I'm telling you the absolute truth in this.) (Galatians 1:16-20 The Message)

Timothy got his instructions directly from God through Christ:

"I didn't receive it through the traditions, and I wasn't taught it in some school. I got it straight from God, received the Message directly from Jesus Christ." (Galatians 1:12 The Message)

This sums up my Maine experience.

~ ~ ~

Another kernel I bring back for deeper consideration is the topic of awareness and sensitivity.

I am growing more and more awareness and sensitivity to myself and others (i.e., I am more aware and sensitive to my bursts of anger that I sometimes subtly dump on Patty). She loves me, accepts me, and forgives me. Now I see it all in new ways, and it transforms my relationship with her.

> "His appearance changed from the inside out." (Mark 9:2-4 The Message)

This defines my Maine experience. My inner transformation spills into exterior changes in how I relate to every person.

~ ~ ~

Is it a truism that the more viability or honor I receive, the greater the temptation to let ego and narcissism motivate my life?

> "Blessed are the meek, for they shall inherit the earth." (Matthew 5:5 RSV)

> "But when you pray, go into your room and shut the door and pray to your Father who is in secret; and your Father who sees in secret will reward you." (Matthew 6:6 RSV)

> "whoever would be great among you must be your servant," (Matthew 20:26 RSV)

The ocean is one of the most powerful forces we know—and it is the lowliest. All waters flow *to* it!

This is all a metaphor for how to *be* unconditional love in our world—the Way of Christ.

Going back to Ken Wilber's philosophy for integral living, the following occurs to me:

- Any religion or political system that is not inclusive is broken.
- Either-or thinking is also broken—the Way of Christ is both-and.
- Postmodern thinkers are both global and integral.
- Each generation builds on the shoulders of the past generations to move toward integral living.

~ ~ ~

I am cosmic energy. My time in Maine has brought forth new growth within me.

I feel more energy, excitement, and motivation for nearly everything.

It's easier to set priorities and live by intention.

Life is so much simpler when we learn to live in the now.

My faith is becoming more vital each day as I learn to live with "God awareness" in each moment.

I feel mostly free of my former compulsions.

It's easier to let go of anger.

I have a new and growing sensitivity to the needs of others.

Prevenient grace has new meaning for me.

I can trust promises of scripture for safety, protection, guidance, provision, and joy—growing my sense of now *and* eternity.

The Bible has come alive for me in a whole new way; all scripture readings are taking on new light and life.

CHAPTER 26

Faith comes from the bottom of the heart.

Another thing I brought back from Maine is a new appreciation and enjoyment of Patty. We have a new relationship in which I discount her much less frequently (I was previously unaware of how many ways I was doing this). We're spending more time together, having more fun, and enjoying a lot of deep, inner dialogue for longer sessions than our previous exchanges of passing thoughts and observations.

It is easier to accept things I used to criticize, to accept her help, and to honor her commitment to me and to others (friends and strangers). I feel a deep and special joy and gratitude that Patty married me and has stayed with me through some very tough times.

I also notice that more of our decisions are now mutual. As I listen to her more deeply, I tap into my deep appreciation for her gifts and creativity. Patty is creative in so many ways—cooking, decorating, caring for others and me, writing, quietness, and service to others (and me), to name a few.

Overall, what I'm finding here at home is a closer walk with Jesus. More than "the only way," he is *my* only way. I return with the conviction that somehow this deeper awareness and understanding is a key to revitalizing the church.

It sure has been for Larry Grubb.

John Bailey (1643–1697) was an English dissenting minister (a leader of protestant Christians who separated from the Church of England in the 17th and 18th centuries), who was imprisoned in England (and then later in Ireland) for his "nonconformity." He was later secretly released on the condition that he left Ireland by a specific deadline, never to return. Because he was not allowed to say goodbye to his followers or preach a farewell sermon, the brokenhearted Bailey said his sorrowful goodbyes in a letter address before making his way to New England, where he remained for the rest of his life.

A short book by Bailey, *Man's Chief End to Glorify God, or Some Brief Sermon-notes on 1 Corinthians,* included this 1689 farewell letter address to his flock. For his funeral sermon he chose for its text the words "into Thy hands I commit my spirit!" (Luke 23:46 RSV) on which Mr. Bailey had prepared a sermon—never delivered—presuming it would be his last.

Perhaps reflecting on the ups and downs of his faith life and ministerial career, Bailey writes, "A vital faith involves the top of our heads and the bottom of our hearts."

After my time in Maine, I now know a little more about both. What I read and study is "top of head." What I learn in silence is "bottom of heart."

It took some time in the stillness of nature to acquire a God consciousness I have not experienced before. What I learned from this is that while God is unknowable, what I *can* know of God comes through intuition, in silence.

In the book, *Living Your Strengths,* authors Albert L. Winseman D.Min., Donald O. Clifton Ph.D., and Curt Liesveld M.Div. M.A write:

> There is something about the concept of talents and strengths that just "feels right." When we discover our talents, when we give them a name, something resonates deep within us. It is as if our spirits react to this discovery with a resounding "Yes! This is the way it is supposed to be—this is who I was created to be." And we find it somehow

freeing; naming our greatest talents sets us free to develop them and live through them. Naming our top talents gives us permission to accept our areas of lesser talent and either discard them or manage them. It gives us permission to stop trying to be who we are not and concentrate on who we are—who we were originally created to be.

This defines Maine for me. We are made for God—in His image. We are made to love—that is God's call.

~ ~ ~

In Galatians, Paul provides insights about his personal breakthrough: "I did not confer with flesh and blood, nor did I go up to Jerusalem to those who were apostles before me, but I went away into Arabia; and again I returned to Damascus." (Galatians 1:13-17 RSV)

In the book, *Authentic Letters of Paul, A New Reading of Paul's Rhetoric and Meaning*, authors Lane McGaughy, Arthur J. Dewey, Roy W. Hoover, and Daryl D. Schmidt, four Jesus Seminar Fellows, combine their scholarship to offer up a very different understanding of Paul and his message. Based on the Greek translation of Paul's writings, this book reflects not on personal guilt, but on the trustworthiness of God and the courageous faith of Jesus in God to create a role model for others.

So, after Paul's transforming experience with Christ, he went *to be alone* to find its meaning. No conversation with others; no approval from Jerusalem. He spent three years processing this new understanding of who God is.

After describing his former behavior as a practicing Jew and observances of Jewish traditions, which he estimates to be beyond that of most of his contemporaries, Paul then describes what happened to him in traditional biblical prophetic language.

Although he sees his experience as a prophetic "call" from God, he never considered himself a convert; he was still a devout, practicing Jew: "For I could wish that I myself were accursed and cut off from Christ for the sake of my brethren, my kinsmen by race. They are Israelites, and to them belong the sonship, the glory, the covenants, the giving of the law, the worship, and the promises; to them belong the patriarchs, and of their race, according to the flesh, is the Christ. God, who is over all, be blessed forever." (Romans 9:3-5 RSV)

Paul's paradigm shift in his understanding of God and the nations moved him beyond his own Pharisaic self-understanding. Embracing the vision of other Jewish prophets in *their* call to the nations, this shift empowered him to set about what he understood to be his new task of announcing this vision and understanding to support a "new chapter of God's action."

After Jesus' call and commission from God he spent 40 days alone in the wilderness: "The Spirit immediately drove him out into the wilderness. And he was in the wilderness forty days, tempted by Satan; and he was with the wild beasts; and the angels ministered to him." (Mark 1:12-13 RSV)

While on his preaching tour of Galilee, many of Jesus' private sessions with God happened in the early mornings: "And in the morning, a great while before day, he rose and went out to a lonely place, and there he prayed." (Mark 1:35 RSV)

When Jesus was in a storm at sea with his Disciples, whom he described as "O men of little faith," he spoke his calm to quiet the stormy seas around them: "And he said to them, 'Why are you afraid, O men of little faith?' Then he rose and rebuked the winds and the sea; and there was a great calm." (Matthew 8:26 RSV)

How does all of this pertain to me? How is it applicable to my time of stillness and solitude in the wilderness, my talks with God before pre-dawn fires, my "little faith" in times of storm, and my new awareness that calms these raging seas?

I went to Maine to examine my faith; I spent three months alone to do this. My desire and my questioning also centered on the church—what should our church and the church of the future look like? How essential is the church for individuals being God's unconditional love? How do we learn how to be?

I learned that while I am well equipped for the "top of my head" faith, as John Bailey, the "dissenting minister," concluded, I know far too little about my "bottom of the heart" faith.

My faith was tested in many ways in Maine. Like Elijah and Isabel, who "lived with wild animals and were safe," I faced risks I wasn't sure I could manage there. My faith allowed me to survive an encounter with a bear. (I later learned there were 37 bears sighted in my campsite area last year and not everyone was so lucky!)

I found deep dependence on Psalms 91 and 103:

> He who dwells in the shelter of the Most High, who abides in the shadow of the Almighty, will say to the Lord, "My refuge and my fortress; my God, in whom I trust." For he will deliver you from the snare of the fowler and from the deadly pestilence; he will cover you with his pinions, and under his wings you will find refuge; his faithfulness is a shield and buckler. You will not fear the terror of the night,

nor the arrow that flies by day, nor the pestilence that stalks in darkness, nor the destruction that wastes at noonday. A thousand may fall at your side, ten thousand at your right hand; but it will not come near you. You will only look with your eyes and see the recompense of the wicked. Because you have made the Lord your refuge, the Most High your habitation no evil shall befall you, no scourge come near your tent. For he will give his angels charge of you to guard you in all your ways. On their hands they will bear you up, lest you dash your foot against a stone. You will tread on the lion and the adder, the young lion and the serpent you will trample under foot. Because he cleaves to me in love, I will deliver him; I will protect him, because he knows my name. When he calls to me, I will answer him; I will be with him in trouble, I will rescue him and honor him. With long life I will satisfy him and show him my salvation. (Psalm 91 RSV)

Bless the Lord, O my soul; and all that is within me, bless his holy name! Bless the Lord, O my soul, and forget not all his benefits, who forgives all your iniquity, who heals all your diseases, who redeems your life from the Pit, who crowns you with steadfast love and mercy, who satisfies you with good as long as you live so that your youth is renewed like the eagle's. The Lord works vindication and justice for all who are oppressed. He made known his ways to Moses, his acts to the people of Israel. The Lord is merciful and gracious, slow to anger and abounding in steadfast love. He will not always chide, nor will he keep his anger for ever. He does not deal with us according to our sins, nor requite us according to our iniquities. For as the heavens are high above the earth, so great is his steadfast love toward those who fear him; as far as the east is from the west, so far does he remove our transgressions from us. As a father pities his children, so the Lord pities those who fear him. For he knows our frame; he remembers that we are dust. As for man, his days are like grass; he flourishes like a flower of the field; for the wind passes over it, and it is gone, and its place knows it no more. But the steadfast love of the Lord is from everlasting to everlasting upon those who fear him, and his righteousness to children's children, to those who keep his covenant and remember to do his commandments. The Lord has established his throne in the heavens, and his kingdom rules over all. Bless the Lord, O you his angels, you mighty ones who do his word, hearkening to the voice of his word! Bless the Lord, all his hosts, his ministers that do his will! Bless the Lord, all his works, in all places of his dominion. Bless the Lord, O my soul! (Psalm 103 RSV)

In addition to these things, the biggest thing I learned in the North Maine Woods is to relax. I have been living for way too long with far too much stress.

And, while I was able to manage the health repercussions of all this stress—diverticulitis, cholesterol, depression—I was still largely unaware of how my lingering stress was telling me, "What you've been doing is not working."

~ ~ ~

Even as I learn more professionally, God is still unknowable. What I *can* know of God comes only through intuition—and silence! Intuition + silence = soul power.

In Maine I acquired a "God consciousness" different from any I've experienced before.

I think if I had tried to explain these things that I now understand so well, post Maine, to my pre-Maine mindset, I would not understand them at all.

How can we really know something we have not yet experienced? We can understand on a theoretical level, sure, but that is different from knowing.

This will be my challenge in sharing my Maine experience with others—teaching and encouraging others to *experience* God rather than just study God.

~ ~ ~

Jesus' ministry was to the poor and forgotten. In the early church, on Paul's second trip to Jerusalem, they affirmed his mission and only requested that he remember the poor: "only they would have us remember the poor, which very thing I was eager to do." (Galatians 2:10 RSV)

I went to Maine to get my eyes and ears opened, for personal transformation—and transformation of Christ's church. My trip to Maine was an attempt to explore what we can do differently—individually and as a church—to get different results.

"All things are full of weariness; a man cannot utter it; the eye is not satisfied with seeing, nor the ear filled with hearing." (Ecclesiastes 1:8 RSV)

Considering all of this, what can *we* do differently? At first it seemed to me that a corporate or committed Christian community dialog is essential to finding these answers. I wasn't in Maine for very long before the "we" in my question changed to "I."

What could "I" do differently to recover Pentecost? I was waiting for "us" to do it. It soon became apparent to me that if the church of Jesus Christ is out of step, then that means *I* am out of step. I am partially responsible for the state of the church.

So, my new question became, "what am I willing to do differently to make the church what God wants it to be?"

Then I spent my next three months in the Maine woods probing *me*.

What are my blind spots?

What change in commitment will I make?

I found considerable discomfort in this approach—as well as a newfound joy and optimism that I *can* make a difference, even if it is small.

CHAPTER 27

Seeing with freshened eyes

ince Maine I see myself, my church, and my world with more honesty, more loving, and humble confessing in our broader and less self-serving ways. I choose each of these descriptive words with careful intention and very deep meaning.

When a couple I know went to the Galapagos islands a few years ago, they brought back pictures of God's amazing, unreal, and unique personality. Seeing those pictures and hearing their stories was wonderful, but it was nothing like being there and seeing it all with my own eyes and hearing everything there with my own ears.

This is the challenge I face in sharing my Maine experience with others, hoping they will find inspiration in the stories of my wilderness wonderings and personal experiences of nature, God's first bible.

How do I define or describe an experience to one who has never been there? How can I possibly convey the wonders of this kind of stillness to those who have never secluded themselves in nature? How many people have (or will create) the opportunity to spend three months in silence?

I worked so hard at it for years and failed. I reluctantly turned it over to God, and it happened in less than one year. But who else with a busy life would be that motivated and determined to spend that much time alone, in complete stillness?

This was a wake-up call for me. Have I been working too long and too hard as a United Methodist minister (67 years) and not done enough listening, obeying, and responding to the Source that created me? I decided, "YES!"

Jesus began his ministry in silence. He listened and strategized for 40 days.

Paul spent three years doing much the same: "But when he who had set me apart before I was born, and had called me through his grace, was pleased to reveal his Son to me, in order that I might preach him among the Gentiles, I did not confer with flesh and blood, nor did I go up to Jerusalem to those who were apostles before me, but I went away into Arabia; and again I returned to Damascus. Then after three years I went up to Jerusalem." (Galatians 1:15-18 RSV)

I was not making room for silence, listening, and seeing with fresher eyes. Was this my problem? Yes. Our church's problem? Probably so. We are working hard and long and getting the same or diminishing results.

In Father Richard Rohr's book, *The Naked Now,* he talks about the idea of *conversion*—helping people clarify subjectivity—as crucial to understanding how mystics "see." Calling upon the famed Jesuit thinker, Bernard Lonergan (1904–1984) and his theories of knowledge and insight, Rohr elaborates: "Conversion is not the exclusive domain of hermits and ecstatics; even brilliant academic theologians have recognized its importance."

Observing that while Christians claim to have total and absolute truth from the beginning, and scientists are willing to work for decades knowing that their theories and hypotheses are merely provisional, Rohr asserts that "the process of conversion was itself the great clarifier and was the healing of our own woundedness, neediness, and egocentricity so that true seeing could be possible, insofar as it is possible." He goes on to say that authentically converted people can then *see* truth in a way that can be shared, at least with other converted people.

"I know how 'safe' and energized I feel when I am sharing even my most offbeat ideas with truly holy or loving people—or good therapists," Rohr says. "You know they will understand what you are searching to say. Among antagonistic, insecure, or dualistic people, you always feel unsafe."

Concluding that humans beings attract other human beings to the same level of awareness, Rohr believes that Lonergan's "new foundation for truth-seeking" gleaned from science is a remarkable breakthrough in the connection between the seer and the seen.

Perhaps this is how we can get beyond the "my ideas versus your ideas" dogmas and learn to "fish for men," as Jesus instructed, *inside* of our religion.

~ ~ ~

Why so much status quo? Rohr asks and answers this question in *The Naked Now:* "Once you know that the one thing the ego hates more than anything else is change, it makes perfect sense why most people hunker down into mere survival."

What can I do, this moment, today, living in the *naked now,* to be "God's person in the world?"

At home shortly after my return, I got up at 5:00 a.m., brewed my coffee, and planned to go for a walk. The now moment said, "Stay still and be." About an hour later, someone I have been wanting to talk with and whose complex schedule and limited time had prevented conversation, calls.

Prevenient grace!

Then, later in the morning I planned to write two insights. The now moment told me to make another phone call that led to a very mutually helpful 45-minute conversation. My desire to write returned after that call, but once again, the now moment said, "Make another call to find a benefactor to underwrite a program that still needs funding." This went on until 10:30 a.m., when I finally got to my writing. But look what all happened I couldn't have predicted if I had not been living (and listening) in the naked now!

~ ~ ~

Divine presence is a gift. We all have it, we cannot control it, and yet it still must be asked for, as we learn in Luke: "If you then, who are evil, know how to give good gifts to your children, how much more will the heavenly Father give the Holy Spirit to those who ask him!" (Luke 11:13 RSV)

In *The Naked Now*, Rohr also explains that this "asking" we must do is really more like *awakening* this gift that already lies within us; it has already been given, whether we realize it or not. He likens most Christians today to the citizens of Ephesus, back in apostolic days recounted in the book of Acts: "And he said to them, 'Did you receive the Holy Spirit when you believed?' And they said, 'No, we have never even heard that there is a Holy Spirit.'" (Acts 19:2 RSV)

The point is, God doesn't force this gift of presence on us—we have to choose to awaken to it. And, while God does provide the *opportunity* for this exquisite dance between our soul and God, we have the freedom to decide what we want to do with that gift.

How can we have this gift and not realize it? That's yet another paradox, says Rohr: "We can't know this gift is within us until after we've awakened it!" Calling faith, "joy-filled hindsight," Rohr adds that the gift of Divine presence is something we learn to trust after we have experienced it during times of risk and varying degrees of darkness. "Henceforth," he assures, "you will remember in the darkness."

~ ~ ~

"Dream dreams, Larry!" The Universe knows how to bring them to fruition if the time has come for these ideas to become reality. How the profound ideas keep flowing my way—and fresh creative ideas bombard me!

I've always been fascinated with the scientific awareness of energetic vibration. Specifically, as it pertains to the human body, science can now track body vibration as it corresponds to our state of health and wellness.

For example, a healthy body vibrates at up to 70 megahertz and will never get sick. When that vibration rate drops to 50-60, we find things like headaches and flu. When it drops to around 42, we find diseases like cancer. And when it drops to 25 or below, death.

Science also now knows that our vibrational frequency attracts and connects to matching frequencies in others. (Have you ever heard the term "misery loves company?") There are there some people it just feels good to be around, and others that, no matter how much you want to connect, it just doesn't feel right. Why do we "click" with some people and not with others, even though all the surface connecting factors appear to line up the same? It's all energy! We're all energy!

And, if this is true for people, could it also be true for ideas? Dreams? Desires? Is this how the Universe brings dreams to fruition? How the time arrives for ideas to become reality? I am reminded of someone who, years ago, told me she wrote and put in her Bible the qualities she wanted to find in her next marriage. Years after she made that list, she found him. He fit the entire list, save one item: he was taller rather than the shorter man she had dreamed of.

~ ~ ~

Another marked change in my attitude is about money. My expanded awareness tells me that my financial support comes from my Source. Not the church, investments, pension, etc., but this new abundance comes in multiple, interior ways:

- the accident avoided;
- a great deal on a car;
- a spouse on the same page on saving; and
- an accident that means insurance will cover unaffordable (but already needed) physical therapy and bodywork.

~ ~ ~

Learning to live in the naked now has created a fresh awareness within me. It calls me to remember to always ask, "God, what is my call in this moment?"

Throughout every day, of the thousands of choices I can make, "Naked Now" has created a fresh awareness that only one choice is the answer to that question. God has given us the software in our hearts to make these choices. Will we remember to use it? When we're uncertain, will we remember to consider:

- Will it bless other people?
- Will it bless me?
- Will it bring comfort?
- Our heart has wisdom far beyond our mind's capacity to know. Here I now find my guide.

~ ~ ~

Post Maine, I am finding myself so much softer and more accepting of myself, Patty, strangers, and enemies. I feel like I've been inoculated with a B12 of Grace.

This feeling is contagious, and it heals relationships, churches, communities, the world, and the cosmos. As I continue to hone my awareness and practice these new behaviors, I am also becoming more aware of my warts. It's always a work in progress!

One of those warts I'm discovering is fear. How much of what we call "evil" is actually created by our own fear? Fear is a messenger, yes, but fear is a messenger that must be managed. Managed well, fear can keep us safe; managed poorly, it can take over and render us incapable of action we need to take. And, when fear becomes our focus, it can create chaos, destruction, and even death. Considering the devastation wrought by fear of "the other," I wonder how much of what we call "evil" is created by fear?

I'm thinking now of my encounter with the bear, and what might have happened if I had reacted in fear rather than sitting calmly and watching him meander by. Had I scrambled for safety (and really there was no such place in my campsite), I might have been tastier than those berries he was focused on.

In some ways my thinking is getting clearer, sharper, and more *realistic* instead of *idealistic*. And, at the same time, more forgetful.

To help me hold onto this peace and focus, I've created a few mantras for living in the "Naked Now:"
"I am peace, God's peace (Jesus' gift)."
"I am freedom, total freedom (Paul's emphasis)."
"I am love, God's unconditional love."
"God is light, healing, loving, peaceful light."

~ ~ ~

The transformation I have experienced and continue to experience as a result of my time in Maine:

Unbalanced idealism transformed to a *maturing realism.*

Unbalanced compulsion transformed to *maturing "now" living.*

From "I have to know or do to be whole" transformed to *"I have all the wisdom, knowledge, cosmic energy, and eternal grace to do anything the Master calls me to BE and DO right now!"*

Things I say and do that are unhealthy transformed to *gratitude for the divine grace to help bring about healthy change.*

Unhealthy, nervous, stressful body movement transformed to *peace, relaxation, and quiet deep within.*

"There is never enough time" transformed to *"I have time for everything that is important for me to do."*

Poverty consciousness transformed to *abundance consciousness.*

Inappropriateness transformed to *sensitivity.*

Narcissism transformed to *altruism.*

Public transformed to *private.*

Assertiveness transformed to *openness.*

Selfishness transformed to *authenticity.*

Conspicuous transformed to *anonymous.*

Action transformed to *inaction when appropriate, and vice versa.*

Fuzzy desire transformed to *sharp intention—do it now and when appropriate.*

My timing transformed to *God's timing.*

Progressing weakness transformed to *health—physically, mentally, and spiritually.*

Getting transformed to *giving.*

Rigid transformed to *spontaneous and flexible.*

Perfection driven transformed to *process driven.*

Complete transformed to *completing.*

~ ~ ~

Here is one very powerful and profound insight I have toyed with in the past and believe now deep in my soul.

Who I am on the outside—to you and to the world—is determined, in God's grace, by who I choose to be on the inside.

I was totally aware of the personal risk I was taking to live in the setting and circumstance I chose for my wilderness retreat. I was at peace with dying, but also held a deep conviction that it wouldn't happen!

My life experiences have taught me, again and again, that the most secure life I can find is in uncertainty and change. This is life in the raw. This is what Jesus taught:

"Whoever seeks to gain his life will lose it, but whoever loses his life will preserve it." (Luke 17:33 RSV) In other words, the only way to find life is to find it in God and in pursuit of God in ever season of life.

There is only one certainty in life as I see it. I was created by God, and this love will sustain me in every circumstance. I only need to follow the truth every great religion invites us to follow, and Jesus especially, to find my true, authentic life.

It is upon each of us to find our own unique path to a vital, alive, faith in our creator. It is a faith for each of us to discover, but only if we say, "I want it."

We find our faith *through* our quest, our journey, to answer this challenge. Books, worship, friends, service to others—all are valuable tools to help us get there. And my journey, my quest, grew out of who I was on the inside—and what I knew I needed.

Sometimes we need to get out of our comfort zone to hear a fresh word from God.

I spent three months out of my comfort zone, deep in the North Maine Woods. I had no communication with the outside world. I had no transportation but my own two legs. I had to depend on newly established relationships in an environment totally foreign to me, in a culture totally different from urban Texas. If I had food, water, transportation, minimal social contact, it was up to me, living isolated and alone, in a forest, 30 miles from supplies. There were no paved roads or electric power lines.

It was life in virgin nature, just as God made it, just like Henry David Thoreau found it 150 years ago. He hired a Native American guide to explore the North Maine Woods. Unforeseen circumstances required me to change locations three times with less than a one-day notice.

It was one of the most transforming journeys I have taken. And it was one of the most affirming things that I could do, both in re-grounding my faith in the old, old story, and in uncovering who God made me to be at my birth, born "in the image of God."

I was out of my comfort zone, totally dependent on strangers to survive for three full months. I wanted to test a faith I had preached for most of my life and seldom was forced to prove.

It birthed a whole new lifestyle; a different quality of daily living; adventure and joy I had not known in the past.

These writings are meant to mature what was birthed on this journey—and to share these insights, life thoughts, observations, and reflections in a way that I hope will feed you, as they have me.

EPILOGUE

Live in the NOW

Before and After:

What changes in me and lessons learned can I share about my Maine experience?

Before: Get disconcerted, see something or someone that didn't fit what I would call "good," and criticize or judge, sometimes in a nasty way.

After: Same scene, much easier to see their positive intent. I am then able to focus on their positive attributes and feel grateful. I realize that it takes much less energy from me to see the positive, accept them as they are, forgive if I have chosen to feel hurt.

Before: See something, push to do it now, because it ought to be done; I won't have to mess with it later. It gets me into "doing" mode, so I don't have to face myself honestly. I don't need or invest in changing me— I'm comfortable as I am! (unaware, lazy, naive, etc.) I see this as a pattern I developed in high school and carried until now.

After: I sat today for probably 10 minutes, just reflecting on different things. Picked up the atlas and studied where I was in Maine. Fixed lunch. I am learning to just flow in the moment, do what I want to, not compelled to by inner habit.

Before: I was in high stress and didn't know it. I had hypnotized myself to think, "I'm so calm and peaceful." Baloney! The moment I sat down I crossed my legs. I often sat, "at peace" in my chair with my arms crossed and over my chest. Or my fingers interlocked on my lap. All positions stress-produced! Sometimes, I even bounced my knees and legs!

After: I still want to cross limbs. The instant I do it or think to do it, I say, "peace, peace, peace," and anchor back to sitting peacefully and silently in the perfect stillness of the wilderness. The moment I uncross any part of my crossed body, I can feel ease and relaxation in my gut, and I feel much calmer. I have more to do here and am habitually checking in with my "truth button"—my gut!

Before: It was an intentional challenge to sit and do nothing. I had to consciously work at it.

After: I sit and do nothing for hours and feel like it has been a few minutes. I can lay in bed for long periods of time, perfectly still, not even wanting to move, examining each part of my body for any feeling of tension.

Before: Reflecting on my church responsibilities, things yet undone, I immediately feel stress in my body and picture in my head what I am going to do.

After: Same scene, I feel relaxed, reminding myself, when necessary, "I do what I can, when I can, flowing in the moment in Fort Worth as I was flowing in the moment in the woods."

Before: Compulsive, "I've got to get back to Maine, one, two, three, or six months at a time! How will I do it?"

After: "It would be nice to return. I will live in the moment: if it happens, fine; if not, fine. Money to do this can also be used missionally!"

Before: I'll do what I can to maintain my church ministry as long as I enjoy it and they want me.

After: I will go anywhere and do anything my authentic self urges! I will do what I do with fire and passion!

Before: Vision of who I want to be and what I want to do recording in my journal how I will do it. Re-read these often until they become ingrained as habit.

After: Vision the same, but then let go and live in the moment!

Before: Control, control, control!

After: Listen, learn, flow, suggest, and accept!

APPENDIX A
STUDY/DISCUSSION QUESTIONS

Out of your own life experience and vision, write your own metaphor for life. In your life's wonderful learning journey, what rich, inspiring, and rewarding experience could you share?

Developing a Listening Heart

"I didn't receive it through the traditions, and I wasn't taught it in some school. I got it straight from God, received the Message directly from Jesus Christ." (Galatians 1:12 The Message)

Discuss!

1. Larry's style of fire building: Start with tinder, dry pine, pinecones, pine needles, then add small twigs, then bigger and bigger sticks, sized 1-2 inches in diameter. Then I place a medium-sized cedar or maple log or limb on top. Next, I make a tipi 1-2 sticks deep all around it, and then light the fire, adding wood from there as I choose. How is this construction a metaphor for how to build a life?

2. While this fire construction is best left alone to catch and burn as it will, frequently the kid in me wants to start messing with the fire—and I usually make it worse. Discuss how this applies to "nature knows best" in your own life.

3. Each morning as I began the day's fire, I become a more exquisite fire builder. The more experienced I got, the better I got! How does this apply to life?

4. One of my early mentors had something I wanted, and I wasn't ever sure what that was. There were many reasons I wanted to be like my mentor, and I identified with many of his ideas, but 42 years later in the wilderness, my mind still puzzled on this, identifying more and more of who he was, rather than what he did, except as what he did reflected who he was! What examples of what we do reflecting who we are can you identify?

5. As I got near the end of my fire for one day, I would pick up multiple hands full of the dry twigs, leaves, and partial branches and throw them on the fire, over and over again, at one time. Doing this led to quite a hot bed of coals beneath my remnant fire. Discuss the metaphors in the life of a church and its community for cultivating such a hot bed of coals that it ignites new fires.

6. For me this is about helping to build a new church, a new disciple group, and new study groups. How can we identify and support the sturdy pieces of wood that will ultimately become the hot, hot coals, nearly invisible, that ignite new branches added before they are gone?

7. If relationships build the fire within each of us, what fuels the fire over time? As the core of the relationship wanes, what can we do to keep the fire from dwindling and even perhaps dying?

8. I love cedar in my fire. It burns well. It crackles, sparks, and I love the smell of burning cedar. And there is a downside! Those sparks also sometimes jump into my wood supply and start another fire. (I keep bucket of water handy to handle this.) Sometimes the sparks hit my bare legs, socks, or pants and burn holes (and burn Larry unless addressed very quickly). Discuss how, no matter how beautiful and delightful our life is, there are always sparks jumping out that can burn us. We must think quickly and respond. How do we respond? Fear? Anger? Love? Unconditional love? We must decide! When

one of these sparks doesn't fit into our program as we envision it, we may criticize, judge, and discount its importance. How do we move to a place of thanking God for each spark—another wonderful awareness to help us learn, prepare adequately, be ready for the next spark, sure to come!

9. I observed a premature maple, perhaps ten feet tall. One branch higher than my reach had been broken off and was hanging by just its bark. Although the limb had many fewer leaves—the young and tender, as well as the big full green leaves, were as healthy as every other leaf on the tree! Discuss how this could be a metaphor of our human family. Even the most broken, most challenged people can flourish and contribute, just as much as anyone else, if not more, in some way unknown to our awareness.

10. As I tend my fire, I want to arrange the wood in "my way" that I think will enhance the fire. Often, when arranged "my way" the wood keeps rolling off. When I give up "my way" and let it lay where it chooses to lay, it enhances the fire more than how I thought it ought to go. How is God's work with us a lot like that?

11. When confronted with a big issue, do we close our journal, read our mail, and say, "I will decide what to do about this later?" We all know, all too well, what that means! How many hundreds of times have we done that? How does unconditional, sacrificial love as Jesus lived answer that question?

12. Here is the sticking point as I see it. Three months revealed to me that the only way to get, really get, the down deep, authentic message, fresh from God, is to get still! Where in our culture today can you do that? We drive too fast; there is too much to do; we don't have a clue how to do it; and to our modern dualist minds, it is completely counterintuitive to do it. Is there a way to overcome this? Jesus and the solid, consistent Biblical message says: "Be still, and know that I am God." (Psalm 46:10 RSV) And God even tries to help: "He leads us beside the still waters." (Psalm 23 RSV) And yet, we keep on living our false assumptions about more, better, and faster. But what else can we do? Where do we go from here? How can we learn to get still in this hurry-up world?

APPENDIX B
JOURNALING PROMPTS

It can be very hard to see our own selfishness (not to be confused with healthy boundaries and renewing self-care—and more related to destructive, narcissistic self-interest).

We often don't see our own controlling. It's important to focus on these questions and ask them of the part of you that knows and understands those things—and then be still enough to hear the answers from within your own being.

How am I selfish?

In what small way can I adjust my selfishness to be more inclusive?

When I sit still and listen, my heart tells me to [fill in the blank] to let go of my fear and allow [what to happen] naturally.

How am I controlling?

What ways can I be more open to nature and Source to allow these things to grow and flourish?

From a perspective of my relationship to [name of group or person], I can release my controlling nature, and [how I can listen or step back to foster the health of the group or person].

What are my challenges?

How are these challenges helping me learn about [fill in the blank]?

Right now, I can [fill in the blank] to change my relationship with [name a specific challenge you've identified].

What are my opportunities?

With regard to [specific task, person, or group], I want to [specify an opportunity and identify your best action].

I feel stuck or stymied about [fill in the blank]. This is a golden opportunity for me to [fill in the blank].

Where are my infinite possibilities; where do I find them?

What is different about infinite possibilities and opportunities?

With regard to [specific challenge], when I open myself to infinite possibilities, I can [note some applications of these possibilities for your challenge].

What or who has shaped my life of spiritual formation? List things that are working and useful to you about what you've learned about your spiritual formation. List things that are no longer useful about what you've learned.

List places and people where you can learn new ideas about your spiritual nature and how you can experiment with them.

Sometimes we may want to dump on God the very things God expects us to take charge of doing—for our own growth. For that reason, saying "I'm helpless, God, you do it for me" may be necessary sometimes.

It bears asking ourselves some questions, though, to see what we're capable of doing and then seek guidance from God (or Source) about the best way to proceed.

Is my challenge with [fill in the blank] a growth opportunity?

What can I do right now to address [your challenge]?

A Simple Prayer:

> *"God (Source), I'd like some guidance about [fill in the blank]. What is the best approach for me to take with this right now?"*

Some may want to say, "It's God's will" as the reason for anything that happens, good or bad. What role do we have in this? How do we create what we perceive as "good" or "bad" in our lives? Looking back on your now life, how did your initial perception of "good" or "bad" align with ultimate outcomes?

Is [state a situation] God's will?

My perceptions about how this is good include:

My perceptions about this is bad include:

One perception I can alter about this is:

Having the patience to ask these questions and explore the answers is part of our darkness. The answers are never that black and white—it's up to us to discover how we create our own experiences and derive ultimate meaning of the "good" and "bad" in our own lives.

BIBLIOGRAPHY/RESOURCES

Armstrong, Karen. *A History of God.* (Knopf, 1993)

Bailey, John. *Man's Chief End to Glorify God, or Some Brief Sermon-notes on 1 Corinthians.* (Samuel Green, Anno. 1689).

Barton, Ruth Haley. *Invitation to Solitude and Silence: Experiencing God's Transforming Presence.* (InterVarsity Press, 2010).

Dawson, George, Glaubman, Richard. *Life Is So Good.* (Random House, 2000).

Dyer, Wayne. *Change Your Thoughts - Change Your Life: Living the Wisdom of the Tao.* (Hay House, 2007).

Eckhart, Meister. *Meister Eckhart: Teacher and Preacher.* (Paulist Press, 1987).

Frissell, Bob. *You Are a Spiritual Being Having a Human Experience.* (North Atlantic Books, 2001).

McGaughy, Lane, Dewey, Arthur J., Hoover, Roy W., Schmidt, Daryl D. *The Authentic Letters of Paul: A New Reading of Paul's Rhetoric and Meaning.* (Polebridge Press, 2010).

Moyers, Bill. "Joseph Campbell and the Power of Myth." (PBS documentary series, 1988).

Newell, John Philip. *Sounds of the Eternal: A Celtic Psalter.* (William B. Eerdmans, 2002).

Rohr, Richard. *The Naked Now: Learning to See as the Mystics See.* (The Crossroad Publishing Company, 2009)

Sanford, John A. *Dreams: God's Forgotten Language.* (HarperOne, 1989).

Tzu, Lao. *Complete Works of Lao Tzu: Tao Te Ching & Hau Hu Ching.* (Sevenstar Communications, 1995).

Wilber, Ken. *A Theory of Everything: An Integral Vision for Business, Politics, Science, and Spirituality.* (Shambhala, 2000).

Winseman, Albert L., Clifton, Donald O., Liesveld, Curt. *Living Your Strengths: Discover Your God-Given Talents and Inspire Your Community.* (Gallup Press, 2004).

Wombacher, Michael. *11 Days at the Edge: One Man's Spiritual Journey into Evolutionary Enlightenment.* (Findhorn Press, 2008).

Yogananda, Paramahansa. *Autobiography of a Yogi: The Original 1946 Edition plus Bonus Material.* (Crystal Clarity Publishers, 2005).

Yogananda, Paramahansa. *Man's Eternal Quest: Collected Talks and Essays.* (Self-Realization Fellowship, 1982).

ABOUT THE AUTHOR

"I enjoy reading and learning new ways to serve people—and squeezing every ounce of joy out of the years I have left to live."

About the Author

Rev. Larry Grubb is a retired pastor who grew up in the Texas Panhandle and western Oklahoma. After graduating from Boise City High School in 1951, he earned a bachelor of arts degree in English from Oklahoma City University in 1955 and a master of divinity degree from Garrett Theological School on the campus of Northwestern University in Evanston, Illinois, in 1959.

After serving for 22 years as pastor of local churches in Oklahoma and Chicago from 1951-1973, Larry became Minister of Counseling at First United Methodist Church of Fort Worth in 1973, where he served full time until his retirement in 1998; he remained on staff there in a part-time capacity for the next two decades.

It was a three-week workshop with Carlisle Marney at the Lake Junaluska Conference and Retreat Center in the Great Smoky Mountains of Western North Carolina that dramatically changed the course of Larry's pastoral career toward a counseling practice that would touch countless lives with his gentle wisdom. This pivotal decision changed the trajectory and impact of Larry's personal, interpersonal, and community accomplishments for the next six decades.

After obtaining what would today be the equivalent of a doctorate degree in transactional analysis, Larry devoted the rest of his pastoral career to counseling and delving into the deepest underpinnings of faith, spirit, and helping others to heal a myriad of hurts of the human condition. Recognizing the strong, symbiotic connections between faith and healing, the power of the subconscious on physical wellbeing, and the mental and spiritual aspects of serious illness, Larry declined numerous offers for private practice and chose instead to keep his counseling within the pastoral framework.

Through the years, his education included training, certification, and work with:

- The Midwest Counseling Center in Oklahoma City, Oklahoma
- The International Transactional Analysis Association
- American Association of Pastoral Counselors
- Graduate work in Clinical Pastoral Education from Phillips University in Enid, Oklahoma
- Psychiatric Ward of the Ponca City Hospital in Ponca City, Oklahoma
- Clinical Pastoral Education at the Bi-State Mental Health Foundation in Ponca City, Oklahoma
- Intensive Clinical Training at the Western Institute of Group and Family Therapy in Watsonville, California
- Advanced Clinical Therapy Training at the Midwest Institute for Human Understanding in Medina, Ohio
- Phase I and II training with the Cancer Counseling Research Center in Fort Worth, Texas
- Ericksonian Hypnosis
- Neurolinguistics
- Gestalt Therapy
- Relationship Building with Inter-Personal Communications Programs, Inc. of Minneapolis, Minnesota
- Phase I and II training with Dr. Vernon Woolf using the Psychomaturation Process
- Pea Mellody on Co-dependency
- Fred Prior Seminars on Conflict Resolution
- Fun and Laughter Workshop with Steven Allen Sr. and Jr. and other nationally known comedians
- Imago Therapy training with Dr. Harvel Hendrix

After joining the staff of First United Methodist Church in Fort Worth, Larry logged thousands of hours as a pastoral counselor in areas of divorce recovery, grief counseling, suicide prevention, support for survivors of suicide, Adult Children of Alcoholics, Samaritan House residential AIDS treatment center, and oncology patient support. Beyond the church, Larry's activities to contribute to the mental health and wellbeing of the community at large included:

- sixteen years on the Board of the Mental Health Association of Tarrant County
- assisting in the formation of The AIDS Interfaith Network and Samaritan House (housing for homeless persons living with AIDS)
- serving as board member for United Community Centers
- leading early-stage Alzheimer's education, sponsored by the Alzheimer's Association
- consultant and board member of The Depression Connection, an agency that provides education and advocacy for people with depression and related illnesses
- co-founder, board member, and facilitator of Suicide Survivors: The Healing Journey After Loss

Backdropped by these experiences and a 40-year career of putting his education, training, and knowledge into practice, *Wilderness Wonderings* taps into Larry's ever-deepening curiosity and desire to find the unique inner stillness that allows us to connect with the Source of our being. Within the pages of this book, readers will find a thoughtful coalescence of this lifetime of insights, bubbling forth with a new sense of purpose.

During his three-month sabbatical in the Maine woods, Larry's personal examination of spiritual, psychological, and universal growth (and his place therein) served to widen and deepen his own understanding of the importance of our connection to the natural world—and how allowing nature to inform us of the essence of our creator can help us to continue to evolve our connection to Spirit and the spirit of other human beings across our planet. About creating *Wilderness Wonderings*, Larry's magnum opus of his life's learnings, questions, and observations, Larry simply says, "I enjoy reading and learning new ways to serve people—and find ways to squeezing every ounce of joy out of the years I have left to live."

Printed in the United States
by Baker & Taylor Publisher Services